ONE MURDER TOO MANY

ONE MURDER TOO MANY

Whitey Bulger and the Computer Tycoon

By Laurence J. Yadon and Robert Barr Smith

PELICAN PUBLISHING COMPANY
GRETNA 2014

The word "Pelican" and the depiction of a pelican are
trademarks of Pelican Publishing Company, Inc., and are
registered in the U.S. Patent and Trademark Office.

Library of Congress Cataloging-in-Publication Data

Yadon, Laurence J., 1948-
  One murder too many : Whitey Bulger and the computer
tycoon / by Laurence J. Yadon and Robert Barr Smith.
    pages cm
  Includes bibliographical references and index.
  ISBN 978-1-4556-1819-4 (hardcover : alk. paper) — ISBN 978-1-
4556-1820-0 (e-book) 1. Wheeler, Roger, 1926-1981. 2. Murder
victims—Oklahoma. 3. Computer industry—Oklahoma. 4. Bulger,
Whitey, 1929- 5. Criminals—Massachusetts—Boston. I. Smith,
Robert B. (Robert Barr), 1933- II. Title.
  HV6533.O6Y33 2013
  364.152'3092—dc23
                                                    2013023858

Printed in the United States of America

Published by Pelican Publishing Company, Inc.
1000 Burmaster Street, Gretna, Louisiana 70053

Contents

On August 12, 2013, James Joseph Bulger, arguably the most significant organized crime figure of the twentieth century, was convicted of planning the murder of eleven people. One of them was computer tycoon Roger Wheeler, a fellow Bostonian who also owned controlling interest in World Jai Alai of Miami, Florida. This is their story.

Prologue

"I've been arrested!" Gasko croaked over a cell phone as the FBI agents watched his every move. Seconds earlier, a neighbor had scolded the officers for the way they surprised and roughed up the old man in the storage area of his seedy Santa Monica apartment complex. She noticed that Gasko seemed ashamed as he looked down at the grimy floor. Soon, Gasko's "wife," Carol, also would be sporting silver bracelets.

When Osama Bin Laden was caught and killed in May 2011, bald, bearded, eighty-something Charles Gasko knew he was in trouble. With Bin Laden gone, Gasko became the most hunted man on America's fugitive list, thanks, he thought, to those rich cake-eaters in Tulsa.

It wasn't much of a life anyway, if one of Gasko's neighbors could be believed. Gasko couldn't lift a laundry basket or keep up with Carol on the Santa Monica boardwalk nearby, or so it seemed. Charles and Carol lived like lower-middle-class pensioners getting by on next to nothing, trapped in four small rooms with bare, bashed-in walls that hadn't been painted in years. They walked around on dirty gray carpet from the 1980s.

But the price was right, thanks to rent control. The Gaskos paid only about $900 per month, a bargain in that pricey city. The place was dark most of the time, thanks to the black curtains covering the windows facing a nearby luxury hotel — that is, when Gasko wasn't window peeping.

Unlike most pensioners, however, the Gaskos had nearly $1 million in cash hidden away in their apartment at the Princess Eugenia complex.

They came for him on June 22, 2011, two days after the FBI rolled out a $2 million reward for the old man's arrest. They offered $100,000 for Carol, almost as an afterthought.

Gasko had been ratted out by Anna Bjornsdottir, Miss Iceland 1974, a neighbor who had noticed how well he had cared for an abandoned cat named Tiger. The day before, she had recognized the Gaskos on television from her summer home in Reykjavík, Iceland, and called the authorities immediately. After all, $2 million is a lot of money.

The tired old man who pretended to be losing a battle against Alzheimer's disease back in Santa Monica wasn't Charles Gasko. His real name was Bulger, which sounded vaguely German or Polish but was actually Gaelic for "yellow belly."

Back in South Boston, they called him Whitey.

Thirty years earlier, the Winter Hill gang assassins drove past the swank Southern Hills Country Club gatehouse in Tulsa as if they owned the place, up the oak-lined road that climbed gently leftward past the championship golf course that Tiger Woods would praise years later. The day was Wednesday, May 27, 1981.

Johnny Martorano and Joe McDonald probably didn't notice the polo fields, skeet-shooting range, or the bare grass, where first-class stables and a riding arena had been before a tragic fire five years earlier. Nor did they care much for the classic architecture or evident attention to detail, right down to the pristine trash cans. The assassins were far too preoccupied with their assignment to appreciate the tidy gardens or the children at the pool basking in the sunlit spring afternoon.

Martorano had killed at least eighteen people by then, many dispatched with a quick pistol shot to the back of the head in cars, trucks, bars, and alleys, often in the company of the victim's friends. Most of the men Martorano killed never knew it was coming, but this time, with Roger Wheeler, president of Telex Corporation and World Jai Alai, it would be different.

A few days before, Martorano and McDonald had flown into Oklahoma City as "Richard Aucon" and "John Kelly." They had rented a car, driven the 120 miles or so to Tulsa, and stayed in a series of mediocre motels. Their last stop was the aging and neglected Trade Winds West, which had once hosted presidential candidates, where they waited for the hit kit containing weapons, bulletproof vests, and assorted goodies to arrive from South Boston. Martorano later claimed that they used detailed information provided by Wheeler's own trusted security chief, former FBI agent H. Paul Rico, to determine where best to assassinate the target.

They also looked for a fast car to steal. The ideal ride could be quickly driven away from the hit and dumped elsewhere to distract authorities while Martorano and McDonald highballed to Oklahoma City in their nondescript rental car. When the bulky hit kit arrived at the Art Deco Tulsa bus station downtown, the killers moved their plan forward. It had been shipped to "Joe Russo," another prolific assassin then working in Boston, perhaps to deflect attention to Russo's bosses in the Sicilian Mafia.

Martorano had decided they could not kill Wheeler at his mansion, at the back of a largely open, seven-acre estate. Witnesses at the house could have easily observed their escape. Nor was it practical to take him out at the Telex Corporation headquarters, high atop a hill surrounded by acres of bare ground. So, they decided to kill him where Wheeler would be most relaxed and least on his guard—after his regular Wednesday afternoon golf game at Southern Hills.

Less than a month later, a Canadian writer visited the scene of the gruesome murder and said, "On the practice tee, scions of Tulsa's moneyed class, blond, each of them, are learning to correct a slice. A golf cart, canopied against the sun, wheels silently down the lush green fairway and stops, depositing a solitary figure clad in white. A dull splash rises from the swimming pool. From the pro shop bright with chrome, one can watch the Cadillacs and Lincolns come and go. Outside, an unmistakable sound, the patricians tread of golf cleats on asphalt. This is Southern Hills Country Club, sheltered preserve of Oklahoma gentry."[1]

Ordinarily, Wheeler played in a foursome and capped the game with a scotch and milkshake in the clubhouse. Today, he quickly showered and joked with golf shop manager George Matson about his score on the way out. His scorecard said that he had shot an eighty-eight and lost five bucks. Wheeler carped, "These boys are killing me."

Earlier that day, Martorano and McDonald had parked a stolen Pontiac at a large apartment complex near the country club and donned cheap disguises purchased at a Tulsa theatrical shop. Now, they scouted the parking lot just behind the swimming pool, found the Cadillac they were looking for, and waited for Wheeler to appear so they could finish the job and fly back to Florida. Today, Wheeler parked on the far southern edge of the asphalt next to a light pole, facing a small, placid pond surrounded by willows. The killers didn't have to wait long. Soon, the trim figure in a gray pinstriped business suit walked briskly out of the clubhouse, past them and towards the Caddy. Wheeler was late for a meeting back at Telex.

Wheeler opened the door and climbed in, but he didn't see or hear Martorano rushing from behind on his left. Martorano testified a quarter-century later that he grabbed the door to keep Wheeler from closing it and shot him between the eyes with a .38 snubnose pistol just as Wheeler jumped — or fell backward — into the seat. The pistol fell apart as it fired, dropping four bullets, but Martorano didn't stop to pick them up, although he did manage to retrieve the cylinder. Or perhaps he left the bullets on or near Wheeler as a stark warning to others, a common occurrence in the underworld.

Once Martorano was back in the Pontiac, McDonald careened eastward out of the parking lot, passing the party barn called Snug Harbor and the tennis courts. After a sharp right turn, they sped beyond the eleventh hole of the golf course and slipped out a back gate into traffic. Although newspapers reported that the pair promptly disappeared, within a few days an anonymous caller told police that a few minutes after the killing, the assassins stopped long enough to pick up a second car on the residential road paralleling the winding contours of Sixty-First Street to the north.

Of course, Wheeler never knew that he'd been taken out on the orders of Whitey Bulger, a thug for all seasons whose sanction of Wheeler's killing became his own downfall. Nor did he know that Bulger had spent most of his life outside prison in South Boston, less than fourteen miles from the streets where Wheeler started his climb to success as a boy in Reading, Massachusetts.

Wheeler braved through those last seconds of consciousness comforted by club manager Dean Matthews but surrounded by curious kids in swimming suits staring at the spectacle, his head nestled inside a gym bag filled with his own blood. He never knew that an assistant district attorney closely resembling his daughter, Pam, would be standing alone nearby just a few hours later in the dusk, watching detectives investigate his murder. Wheeler may have wondered how in the world he ever thought he could buy a cash business ready-made for Whitey Bulger and other Irish gangsters, whose traditions were centuries old, say no to the skim, and live to tell the tale.

Yet, the fate he unwittingly fashioned for himself had been there all along, obscured by the brightness of a late spring afternoon but mostly hidden by his own unbridled confidence: the specter of violent, lonely death and destiny in a cheap, fake beard, with sunglasses hiding lifeless eyes, rushing into his face from out of nowhere, from behind his own blind spot.

ONE MURDER TOO MANY

Wheeler's automobile after the murder.

Chapter 1
Skin Against Stone

Of his kind, Roger Wheeler was not, perhaps the prototype but the classic form: an aggressive, hard-nosed, shrewd and tireless entrepreneur, with an instinct for making deals. He made them constantly; as other people are into yoga or cooking, Wheeler was into money. Like Gatsby, he was never quite still, oil, gas, real estate, computers, jai alai, refrigerators. The products were immaterial; it was the profit that counted. Getting and spending, his life was defined by numbers; annual revenue, interest rates, lines of credit, cash flows, personal worth. In ways not yet understood, Wheeler's death too — police believe — was ruled by numbers. Said a friend, who was not surprised by the murder, "He just stood up the wrong guy."[1]

The crime scene was unusual to say the least, this being the most exclusive country club in Oklahoma and one of the finest golf courses in the world. Wheeler's dark blue Cadillac sat, forlorn, next to a street lamp on the asphalt. The air pressure on the tires was low, but that mattered little to the detectives processing the scene.

Michael T. Huff, then the youngest-ever Tulsa homicide detective, was one of the officers who caught the case. Sgt. Roy Hunt, an old-style police sergeant who kept a bottle of whiskey in his desk, had said to Huff, "This is gonna change your life. Are you sure you wanna do this?" In the end, Huff said yes, but, according to his own account, his experience at that point was so limited that he only brought three things to the investigation: persistence, unrelenting energy, and purpose. He was willing to go anywhere, do anything, ask any question.

The first weeks of the Wheeler murder investigation were difficult, but things only got worse. Resources were not the issue. An eleven-man task force quickly was appointed to investigate the murder. Nor was there any mystery about what had happened. Wheeler had played golf on Wednesday for the past twenty years with other self-made men or the sons of such men. He had a regular foursome, consisting of Evans Dunn, who owned a drilling company; Robert Allen, who owned a charter bus company; and Thomas Gail Clark, board chairman of the local Beechcraft distributorship. Detective Huff and the other officers learned that their last game together on Wednesday, May 27, 1981, ended at about 4:30 p.m.

After a quick shower, Wheeler bounded down the hill and was getting into his car just west of the crowded swimming pool when the killer approached. He shot Wheeler once in the face at close range and dropped four unfired cartridges. A witness reported that Wheeler was found spread across the front seat of the Cadillac with his feet hanging outside. Flash burns later were found on his arm but not on his face, indicating that he was shot at close range. Witnesses reported that the shooter jumped into a late-model Pontiac or Ford, which some said had an Oklahoma tag with the initials ST or ZT followed by the number 510. At the time of his death, Wheeler had $996 and eight credit cards in the pocket of his blue pinstriped suit.

But what was the motive? No one was more shocked than the members of Wheeler's foursome. "Gail [Clark] and I were still in the locker," Evans Dunn reported. "Robert [Allen] had already gone and Roger had already left. All of a sudden a boy ran in and said someone had been shot." Dunn believed that Wheeler lived for about ten minutes after the shooting, but there was nothing to be done. Allen commented that "it was just like the pope, just like the president . . . Roger did a lot of good for people that he never talked about."[2]

The Roger Wheeler murder scene. (Courtesy Polaris Images)

Police didn't know which of the four Southern Hills exits the assailants took. One witness described the shooter as a Kenny Rogers "look-alike, but dark complexioned with hair over his ears and a full beard. His black hair is streaked with gray." Witnesses to Wheeler's murder remembered that as many as four men were in the car. The shooter was a white man about six feet tall weighing about 200 pounds. Wheeler's business associates didn't have a clue as to who might have killed him.

Telex general counsel Jack Bailey, who had worked with Wheeler for about sixteen years, said that the shooting "was a complete mystery." Bailey recalled, "He asked me to have some things ready for him at 4:30. I was waiting for him when I heard about it. I'd say shock is an understatement of my feelings."[3]

Wheeler's "employees and relatives thought he was a great man, but many businessmen he dealt with thought otherwise" related future sheriff Stanley Glanz, who described him as "a hard-nosed businessman."

Minutes before the shooting, Wheeler had been joking with the golf shop manager, George Matson. "He was very jovial," Matson said, "We were kidding about his golf scores." Among the eye witnesses was the young daughter of a member who watched the killing from the swimming pool diving board. Anonymous wags said that Wheeler enjoyed gambling, but according to one member of his foursome, their weekly golf games rarely involved more than a few dollars and scores weren't kept all that well.[4]

The homicide squad tried to find a local enemy or bad business deal that might have motivated someone to kill Wheeler, but almost from the start, Wheeler's connection to Miami-based World Jai Alai stood out as the leading prospect for solving the case. WJA Inc. was a privately owned corporation founded by Bostonians in the 1920s with operations in Connecticut and Florida. After seeing the sport in Havana, Cuba, the founders bankrolled the legislative campaign in Florida to legalize it.[5] WJA was the nation's largest such enterprise.

World Jai Alai: A Dangerous Game

The game jai alai resembles racket ball, but players use a long, funnel-like scoop to catch and then release a ball into play. The teams are professionals paid out of the betting proceeds, making the sport perpetually ripe for corruption. The ball, known as the *pelota,* is the hardest ball used in any sport and is roughly three-fourths the size of a baseball. The core is made from Brazilian rubber layered with nylon, on top of which two goat-skin covers are tightly pressed and stitched. Usually, the *pelota* has a shelf life of about twenty minutes, due to the high velocity at which jai alai is played. In addition, the ball travels with such dizzying speed that career-ending injuries are not unusual. At least four players have been killed playing jai alai since the 1920s.

The *Tulsa World* reported that Wheeler had acquired World Jai Alai in 1979 (a year later than the actual purchase) for $50 million. By 1981, World Jai Alai had revenues of $150 million and earnings of $12 million. Although Wheeler was reluctant to give interviews about his jai alai interests, in 1979, he wise-cracked to a *Miami Herald* reporter he brushed off, "I have enough golf buddies." He also related, "I feel comfortable surrounded with FBI types. We have six in the company here."[6] When briefly interviewed by a Miami reporter in 1980, he expressed fear that a lengthier interview might expose him to kidnapping and asked that the reporter note in his story that he employed several former FBI agents.[7]

Not long before he was killed, Wheeler had to appear before the Connecticut Gaming Division board because of concern about his potential partnership in a summer jai alai operation with an associate of prominent underworld figure Meyer Lansky, upon whom the *Godfather II* character Hyman Roth was based.[8] Although the Board approved Wheeler's application for a license, he quickly sold that interest to veteran jai alai careerist Stanley Berenson.[9]

While being vetted for a WJA fronton in Connecticut, Wheeler asked a state investigator, "Are these people I'm involved with, are they reputable people?" The investigator, Dan Twomey, was surprised by the question. "You didn't buy into a church, you bought into a gambling facility. If bad guys can buy into a facility, they will." Despite this, shortly before his death, Wheeler told someone that the New York Stock Exchange was a greater gamble than jai alai.[10]

Shortly after the murder, World Jai Alai officials John B. Callahan and H. Paul Rico, a retired FBI agent, became a person of interest to the Tulsa police. Rico became the most controversial suspect in the Wheeler murder. One wonders how Wheeler could not have known before he bought World Jai Alai that a 1978 Florida gaming official report described Callahan as "an associate of persons believed by the law enforcement community to be organized crime figures." Connecticut gaming officials were also suspicious. Still, this was 1978—the then-rudimentary Internet was a still an academic science project. The due diligence searches, now routinely conducted before corporate acquisitions, were rare and, when conducted at all, seldom more than perfunctory.

Even though the press had previously reported that Wheeler's jai alai interests were among the few in the country not controlled by organized crime interests, the *New York Times* reported eight days after the assassination that First National Bank of Boston, with whom both Telex Corporation and Wheeler himself had a relationship, engaged in "unusual arrangements and financing" for the Wheeler loan. Gaming regulators indicated that "the bank persuaded a reluctant Mr. Wheeler to buy the jai alai company because it was a real money making machine" but then structured the loan agreement to give itself a $1 million financial services fee, which Wheeler complained about but paid. Speculation ensued due to reports of Wheeler firing the three top WJA financial officers in 1980, despite the objections of former WJA president John Callahan.[11] Meanwhile, Wheeler's connection with First National Bank of Boston was both business and personal.

The commitment fee that Wheeler paid was split with Continental Illinois Bank of Chicago, which collapsed a year later for unrelated reasons having to do with Oklahoma oil investments. The loan also restricted Wheeler's flexibility, but he later managed to modify some of the restrictions. Wheeler was, according to the *Times,* caught between "the unorthodox finances of gambling [operations] and the vexing intrusions of FNBB."[12]

David McKown replaced Tom H. Lee, the original WJA account manager who handled the first WJA loan in 1973, at First National Bank of Boston. In 1976, WJA discussed a potential buyout with "two organized crime connected suitors," but the negotiations went nowhere.

As early as 1976, McKown approached Wheeler, who had been considering purchase of the Shenandoah Corporation, which owned two West Virginia racetracks. McKown, vice president of the FNBB energy division, began a lending relationship with Telex in 1971 and managed some of Wheeler's personal energy investments. Wheeler later testified that he purchased WJA despite his misgivings because of McKown's "ecstatic" view of WJA as a "real money making machine." McKown capped the deal by throwing in representation from FNBB legal counsel.

When the deal closed, Wheeler's WJA Realty bought Hartford Jai Alai and its parent WJA of Tampa. WJA Realty now owned four frontons in Florida and Connecticut operations at Bridgeport, Hartford, and Milford.

Three unusual restrictions were attached to the $33 million First National Bank line of credit, which enabled Wheeler's Oklahoma-based WJA Realty to close the deal. First, Wheeler had to keep Richard P. Donovan, the incumbent World Jai Alai president. Second, as a practical matter, Donovan could only be replaced by John B. Callahan, a 275-pound Yale graduate and CPA connected to organized crime.[13] Despite appearances, there is no evidence that the First National Bank of Boston knew then of the Callahan-Winter Hill gang relationship.[14] Third, FNBB loan documents prevented Wheeler from changing the nature of the business or any equity distribution. Thus, the *New York Times* theorized, Wheeler received significant tax sheltering opportunities from the deal, but little else.[15]

Florida, That Sunny Place for Shady People[16]

As time went on, more details about the private World Jai Alai emerged. In December 1974, a faction of the WJA board that wanted to expand operations had forced Pres. J. Stanley "Buddy" Berenson out of office and hired John B. Callahan to replace him. By early 1976, Callahan had applied to Connecticut authorities for permission to construct a fronton in Hartford.

When WJA applied for a Connecticut license in 1976, Gov. Ella Grasso was hardly enamored of the idea. She ordered a state prosecutor with experience investigating corrupt practices and a state police detective to meet with Callahan. Callahan unexpectedly walked out halfway through the meeting, claiming he had to catch a "shuttle back to Miami." The detective easily discovered that there was no such shuttle.

Instead, Callahan bee-lined to Boston, where he met Winter Hill associate Jimmy Martorano (Johnny Martorano's brother), and two wise-guy hangers-on at the Playboy Club. Within a few months, Connecticut law enforcement had conducted enough surveillance at the Playboy Club and Chandler's, the South End restaurant owned by Howie Winter, to disqualify Callahan as the president of WJA for Connecticut licensing purposes due to his association with underworld figures.

At the public hearing, H. Paul Rico, the World Jai Alai security chief and retired FBI agent, appeared in Callahan's stead to report that Callahan had resigned from WJA to "pursue other interests." Later, some suspected that sources within the Boston police department had alerted Callahan.[17] This presented Alan Trustman, the then-leader of the WJA board of directors, with a dilemma. Trustman was a highly successful practicing attorney who wrote movie scripts in his spare time—but this was not play acting, and Trustman had to find new talent, and quick, or face the prospect of losing the Hartford fronton. H. Paul Rico stepped into help.

The first candidate Rico found was Jack B. Cooper, whom the Florida courts had deemed "technically licensable" to operate frontons in that state. However, it didn't take Connecticut authorities long to discover Cooper's ties to Meyer Lanksy. After adverse publicity made the Cooper deal impossible, Bally Manufacturing Corp. made a bid but was likewise eliminated due to alleged organized crime ties.

The exasperated WJA board of directors turned to David McKown of the First National Bank of Boston. McKown knew that Roger Wheeler of Tulsa had $10 million in profit burning a hole in his pocket from a recent deal.

And so, Wheeler entered the picture as owner of World Jai Alai. According to Wheeler's son Larry, by early 1980, Roger Wheeler could see that WJA was not working out. Even though the total amounts bet at the south Florida frontons, called "the handle" in betting parlance, were rising, gross revenues were declining. In the face of this, his deal with First National Bank of Boston obligated Wheeler to retain Donovan and Rico, both of whom he suspected as being the source of the financial problems. Wheeler had discovered that someone was skimming $1 million per year from World Jai Alai. He planned to fire the top financial personnel, do a financial audit, and bring in state officials.[18]

Although Wheeler was initially confident that WJA security officer H. Paul Rico could keep organized crime out of the business, he felt the need for a proper audit.[19] Wheeler also quizzed Miami WJA cashier Peggy Westcoat about the finances. In December 1980, Westcoat and her live-in boyfriend were murdered in Dade County, Florida. Prompted by this and other concerns, Wheeler put the Hartford WJA fronton up for sale.

In 1980, Wheeler told the Rice University Alumni newspaper that he invested in World Jai Alai "simply to make money."[20] His friend Howard Upton agreed with this assessment, but another claimed that World Jai Alai was a tax write-off. He previously had attempted to acquire Shenandoah Corporation, which, according to a 1978 report, owned two horse racetracks and a hotel. At that time, Wheeler reportedly had little interest in jai alai and rarely visited the facilities.[21]

Naturally, Wheeler had kept his options open, and one option was a sale of WJA to outsiders. He told his sons Larry and David that he had a handshake deal with the then-prominent investment-banking firm Drexel Lambert to sell WJA for between $47 and $50 million. Yet, he told his sons, every time he moved towards closing, WJA revenues inexplicably nose dived. Of course Richard Donovan also wanted to buy the company, Larry Wheeler recalled, but Donovan only offered $16 million.[22] According to retired Tulsa homicide detective Mike Huff, shortly before his death, Roger Wheeler told his son David that if he could find Donovan, he would fire him. Shortly before his death, Wheeler reportedly asked Rico to take a polygraph test. Rico refused.[23]

Inquiries from Connecticut state investigators about possible organized-crime influence at Hartford prompted Roger Wheeler to install surveillance equipment on his Telex telephones in Tulsa. He even told one Connecticut investigator that he would authorize tapping Donovan's office phone in Florida. The investigator recalled that Wheeler seemed disappointed to learn that such a wiretap would be illegal.

In early 1981, Wheeler sold the Hartford fronton to former WJA president J. Stanley "Buddy" Berenson — the same man whom John B. Callahan had replaced in 1976. According to then-chief state attorney Austin McGuigan, Berenson soon discovered a big skimming operation. This was consistent with reports by a catering manager that financial statements at the Connecticut fronton showing profits were altered by WJA headquarters in Miami to show losses.[24]

By March, Wheeler was openly nervous. Although months earlier, when boarding his Learjet in Tulsa for trips to Miami, he wisecracked, "I hope they don't bomb my plane today," Wheeler had learned before his flight on March 2 that Rico had called asking about his schedule. Not only did he have his pilot Bill Baggett inspect the plane for bombs, but he also ordered Baggett to take the plane up to cruising altitude on a test flight before boarding with his wife and lawyer.

Earlier, Wheeler had assigned his son Larry, an accounting graduate of Rice University, to examine the WJA books and another son, David, to assess whether there had been a computer scam at WJA, perhaps involving kickbacks or overbilling. Years later, Larry recalled encountering surly employees during an initial anonymous visit to the Miami WJA fronton. He was served a thin, barely digestible steak and a brown salad in the fronton restaurant while H. Paul Rico, whom Larry recognized from photographs, feasted nearby on a thick, well-prepared sirloin with all the trimmings. During the week of Monday, May 18, 1981, about a week before he died, Roger met Larry and David Wheeler at the family ranch in Wyoming to assess the World Jai Alai investment. Wheeler told his sons that he planned to fire Rico and Donovan, who seemed to sense that "something was coming."[25]

The Murder Investigation Begins

The Telex Corporation board of directors met the Friday after the shooting and elected S. J. "Steve" Jatras to replace Wheeler as chairman. Four days after the murder, the *Tulsa World* reported "although newspapers and police in both Tulsa and Florida have connected jai alai with organized crime . . . investigations have failed to associate [Wheeler] with any known crime figures."[26] It was now apparent to all that the Wheeler murder would not be quickly solved.

That same day, a grand jury in Connecticut, which had recommended charges of game fixing two years earlier in late 1979, reconvened in light of the 1981 Wheeler murder. The 1979 Connecticut grand jury found WJA game-fixing had occurred in 1977, but a nine-month investigation revealed no connection between Roger Wheeler and organized crime.[27] In fact, Tulsa detective Roy Hunt quoted a Connecticut investigator as saying Roger Wheeler "was so clean, it scared him."[28]

A month after the murder, the *New Republic* reporter Nicholas Von Hoffman wrote that, in view of Wheeler's murder, the business community was asking itself exactly how good of a bet gambling was.[29]

Curious investigative reporters now began examining World Jai Alai. That June, *Sports Illustrated* reported that John B. Callahan had been ousted from WJA after Boston police tipped Connecticut authorities about his organized crime connections. Still, *Sports Illustrated* reported, Callahan continued to cast his shadow on the organization. *Sports Illustrated* also discovered that Richard P. Donovan had been Callahan's consulting firm partner. WJA sought a buyer but rejected buyout overtures by Callahan and Jack B. Cooper, who was often associated with Meyer Lansky. Cooper had been introduced to WJA officials by H. Paul Rico, Callahan's hand-picked security chief. WJA partnered with three Florida dog tracks, one of which Cooper owned in part.

While Wheeler's Connecticut license application was pending, WJA president Richard Donovan had described Wheeler as "a very wealthy, totally independent guy." But after Florida authorities adjudged Wheeler's moral character acceptable, they were displeased to be told that, as Donovan put it, "Roger would do the deal and he would be gone," implying that Wheeler would be an absentee owner. McKown later testified under oath at a deposition that if the bank named Donovan's successor, his first choice would be Callahan.

Despite misgivings about Callahan's links with Howie Winter of the Boston area Winter Hill gang (his last name was pure coincidence), the sale to Roger Wheeler in June 1978 was approved by Florida authorities, partially because of McKown's assurance that Callahan wouldn't be involved in WJA. Four months later, the Connecticut Commission on Special Revenue (later re-named the Gaming Policy Board) approved the Wheeler acquisition. There was one dissenter. Lester B. Snyder, a University of Connecticut law professor, questioned the role of FNBB in the deal as well as Callahan's influence. The Cooper connection, however, was judged too remote to deny Wheeler a license, especially since there were four companies that had established the summer jai alai operation in Miami, and Cooper was only a partner in one of them.

Wheeler himself claimed at the time of his acquisition that despite concerns about WJA's reputation, the sport was "clean as a hound's tooth." He later assured one reporter, "I've staked my reputation and money on it." Yet, shortly after the Wheeler purchase closed, a grand jury examined allegations of corruption at Hartford and the two other frontons. Ultimately, seven people were convicted of game fixing. Circumstances pointed to inside information being provided to professional gamblers with underworld connections. *Sports Illustrated* later noted that less than three weeks after Wheeler's death, Callahan and his protégé Richard Donovan had a falling out.[30]

Wheeler began focusing in depth on the WJA problems in early 1981. That March, he fired some ten WJA employees after selling the Hartford fronton to Stanley Berensen, a squeaky-clean Boy Scout type, who had complained to the FBI about Callahan and Donovan. First National Bank of Boston later claimed that its WJA dealings had been with people of "sound reputation," referring to the likes of Callahan.[31]

After Wheeler's death, Callahan denied "any involvement whatsoever with organized crime." Perhaps he'd forgotten about his friends in South Boston. The press found more information about the rotund accountant, initially hired by the descendants of the Bostonian founders on a two-year contract. After high school, he joined the Air Force, just as Whitey Bulger had done. Callahan briefly attended Yale in order to learn Chinese. He graduated with a degree in accounting from Bentley College and began working in his father's wholesale produce company in Charlestown, Massachusetts, which at that time had at least as many Irish mobsters as South Boston. Callahan went to work for major accounting firm Ernst & Ernst and then moved to an even bigger firm, Arthur Anderson. He became a partner but left in 1972 under a bit of a cloud. Co-workers commented that he came in late and was often disheveled. Callahan did not seem to have the degree of focus necessary to be a partner.

Two years into his own consulting practice, World Jai Alai hired him to find and recruit a new president capable of expanding company operations into other states. He eventually recommended himself. Of course, Callahan didn't tell the board about his connection to Winter Hill leaders James Joseph "Whitey" Bulger, his underboss Stephen Flemmi, their low-level associate Edward Brian Halloran, or the countless rounds of after-hour drinks he bought at Chandlers in the South End, one of the Winter Hill hangouts.

Callahan then recruited H. Paul Rico as World Jai Alai vice president in charge of security. Rico, who shared Callahan's fascination with organized crime, had retired from the FBI in 1974 and moved to Florida.

Callahan, and perhaps Rico, began the skim. As much as $1 million per year reportedly disappeared from the gross receipts for parking, concessions, and bets. When Callahan was forced out of World Jai Alai in 1976, he left both Rico and consulting partner Richard Donovan in place. Two months later, Callahan tried to buy the company for $35 million but was rebuffed.

One source theorizes that even after he left WJA, Callahan used his contacts to recruit Wheeler as a white knight to buy the company. This would kill three birds with one stone:

pacifying the board, distracting law-enforcement officials concerned about his mob connections, and preserving the skim operation.

David McKown, Callahan's contact at First National Bank of Boston, enticed Wheeler with publicly reported net profits of $5 million on $31 million in gross revenue. The majority interest in World Jai Alai would cost him $50 million, $33 million of which First National Bank of Boston would finance.[32]

After closing the deal, Wheeler immediately became curious when the cash flow did not meet expectations. According to one version of events, when Wheeler discovered the scheme, Callahan turned to an old South Boston buddy who owed him a favor.

The Black Rose

Two years earlier, in 1976, when John Martorano was indicted with other Winter Hill members for fixing horse races, it was Callahan who set him up with a place to hide in Florida, car and all. So Callahan pitched Martorano the first part of the deal: if Callahan bought World Jai Alai, he wanted Winter Hill to provide protection of the skim. According to Martorano, the problem was that if Wheeler, his sons, or accountants confirmed the skim, the complicity of H. Paul Rico and Callahan would be exposed, thus ending the skim and revealing everyone else. Martorano got the go-ahead on the $10,000 per week protection angle from Bulger and Flemmi.

Callahan discussed the rest of the deal personally with Bulger and Flemmi in the Black Rose, an Irish hangout next to Faneuil Hall Marketplace in the heart of Boston.

As Irish Republican Army ballads blared in the background, Callahan had to whisper the second part of the deal to Whitey and Steve. Roger Wheeler would have to be killed so that Callahan could buy World Jai Alai from his wife, Patricia Wheeler, on the cheap. Martorano had already agreed to do the assassination with Winter Hill wheelman Joe McDonald if Whitey and Steve sanctioned it.

But Whitey Bulger was underwhelmed.[33] He was especially put off by Callahan's drinking. Bulger thought that Callahan had some nerve to ask for a hit on a civilian unassociated with the crime business, but later, according to Flemmi, when H. Paul Rico assured Steve that this was a good business opportunity, Whitey began to weaken in his resolve to turn down Callahan's proposal.

Winter Hill gang boss Steve Flemmi wore Bulger down with the dubious claim that Martorano would murder Wheeler anyway, whether Whitey and Steve were in or out.

"I want you to be part of this," Rico had assured Steve later — or so Flemmi said. Whitey's qualms about killing a civilian were only exceeded by fear of the potential blowback. "The guy [Wheeler] is a zillionaire. His family's politically connected. We'll never survive it."[34] Even after giving in, Whitey, whose breath was so bad his associates didn't know whether to offer him gum or toilet paper, predicted the outcome: "We're all gonna go to jail. This will never go away, never."[35]

The Search for Suspects

Within days of Roger Wheeler's May 1981 assassination, Telex Corporation offered a sixty-day, $100,000 reward and launched a nationwide advertising campaign thirteen days later. Telex hired private detectives Jim Bearden and C. T. Burney from Dallas as well as Gary Glanz of Tulsa to solve the murder case. By July 2, Glanz was the only one left working the case.[36] In August, Telex extended the reward for another ninety days as they operated separate telephone banks from those of the Tulsa police department.

Meanwhile, the probate of Wheeler's estate started

routinely enough. Roger Wheeler's will, executed on May 16, 1980, left his home and all his personal belongings to his wife. His daughter, Pamela Kendall Wheeler, and eldest son, Roger M. Wheeler, Jr., were appointed special administrators pending a June 12 hearing. The will directed that both the two children and Continental Illinois National Bank and Trust Company serve as permanent administrators. The balance of his estate was left to be managed by Continental Illinois. Assets included the Wheeler Oil Company and WJA Realty, a limited partnership in Tulsa that owned World Jai Alai in Tampa, Florida, which in turn owned 25 percent of a summer fronton in Miami.[37]

Callahan did not succeed in his efforts to purchase WJA, despite what he had told Martorano, Flemmi, and Bulger.[38]

Authorities discovered that Wheeler controlled dozens of corporations across the country, from Massachusetts to Connecticut to Florida to Oklahoma to Nevada. Often, these were dormant organizations through which assets would be passed.[39]

Adding to the mystery was the baseless rumor that Wheeler had been murdered by Russians. Although the Licensintorg Trading Company of Russia claimed that the Roger Wheeler estate owed it $1 million, there was no evidence at all of criminality. Licensintorg claimed that Wheeler's American Magnesium Company and its partners were obligated to buy magnesium-processing technology for $1 million plus royalties, but the companies eventually resolved the dispute.

By the end of 1981, the *Daily Oklahoman* reported three leading theories for the murder: a botched kidnapping, a foiled robbery, or a hired killing.[40] Police speculated in June 1981 that Wheeler may have been shot in a kidnapping attempt; Oklahoma has a history of such cases.[41] During the Depression, Machine Gun Kelley and his wife kidnapped Charles Urschel, one of the richest men in Oklahoma. Only seven years before Wheeler was killed, Walt Helmerich, scion of a major Tulsa company, had been kidnapped for ransom money on his way to work.

Roger Wheeler had employed six retired FBI agents at WJA, but none of them acted as bodyguards, according to Richard Donovan, WJA president, who said, "I guess I've known Roger Wheeler for going on five years, and I've never known him to have a bodyguard." Wheeler, however bought a personal gun just months before his murder.[42]

As time went by, more details about Wheeler's reason for buying World Jai Alai emerged. Wheeler had been in the market for businesses that threw off cash — and lots of it. He had been told that WJA was all of that and more, spewing out about $6 million ($14 million value in 2013) more than operating expenses every year.

Acquaintances and family members opined years later that Wheeler may have known about connections between organized crime and WJA before he made the deal. After all, it was unlikely that such an astute businessman could have missed or ignored how close the Connecticut jai-alai operation was to several organized crime centers such as Boston, New York, and Philadelphia. Other sources, principally newspaper and magazine accounts, reported years later that Wheeler did not understand or appreciate the risk of mob interference in WJA until it was too late, after he was on the hook for some $50 million. According to these accounts, it was only then that he discovered that his profits were being skimmed.

But in the mid-1970s, when Wheeler first looked at making the investment, jai alai was a bargain for the budget-minded bettor. "Two dollars will buy you fifteen minutes of jai alai, a bargain as compared with a two-minute dog or horse race," said WJA official L. Stanley "Buddy" Berenson, whose father had spearheaded Florida legalization of pari-mutuel betting in 1935.

By December 1976, according to later press reports, World Jai Alai had captured Wheeler's attention. His Oklahoma-based

Phoenix Resources, Inc., reportedly tried to acquire WJA for $54 million in 1976.[43]

The 1977 Bidding War

Seven months later, Wheeler was in a bidding war for World Jai Alai. On July 25, WJA Realty offered $54 per share for WJA, partially in cash, competing against XCor International, a pinball and vending machine manufacturer once known as Seeburg Industries, which had offered $83 million in securities. The main difference between the competitors was the governmental pre-approval of WJA Realty, which had already received licensing from the Florida Pari-Mutuel Wagering Office, following a five-month investigation of Roger Wheeler. Similar clearance from Connecticut gaming authorities was expected.

By the spring of 1980, trouble had emerged at World Jai Alai. During the week of June 4, a special prosecutor of the Connecticut chief state attorney's office obtained warrants to arrest a player and three gamblers on charges of rigging games two years earlier at Milford, Connecticut.

Roger Wheeler, who had a reputation for honesty, had purchased World Jai Alai two years earlier. *Sports Illustrated* reported that "Paul Rico, who was and is [WJA] vice-president in charge of security . . . also attempted to get Jack Cooper of Miami Beach, an associate of mob boss Meyer Lansky to buy World Jai Alai. A former [WJA] president, John Callahan, had underworld associates."

Florida authorities claimed that jai alai was the cleanest pari-mutuel in the country—until investigators discovered gambling "irregularities" in all ten Florida frontons. The potential for irregularities went well beyond Florida. ". . . When you have the same group operating in Rhode Island, Connecticut, and Florida, there are all kinds of opportunities for fraud," the article noted. Reporters Nancy

Williamson and Robert Boyle opined that state officials had everything to gain in the way of tax revenues by looking the other way as betting irregularities flourished.

Fourteen hundred miles to the north, Lester Snyder, who once served on the Connecticut State Commission on Special Revenue, described the basic flaw in jai alai, saying, "the state [Connecticut] is in gambling to make money and therefore the state will never regulate it properly. Abuse will prevail." And so it did, until, at long last, law enforcement authorities challenged a gambling ring called the Miami Syndicate, which took in millions in rigged games at the Milford, Connecticut, fronton in 1977. The Connecticut commission pursued a quartet of alleged jai alai fixers and an aging Spanish player until they were all charged with game rigging and conspiracy to rig games. At the time, jai alai was legal in Florida, Rhode Island, and Nevada. Some fifteen states and two Canadian provinces were then considering adding it to their legalized gambling portfolios.

New Jersey state senator David Friedland then called for legalized betting. Friedland claimed that the state income from pari-mutuel betting would "be dedicated to helping the elderly and the medically and physically handicapped." Of course, the politicians did not match this clamor for funds with regulatory zeal.

Sports Illustrated reporters noted that in 1977 ". . . too many politicians who are at best idealistic and at worst crooked have been overseeing the game." In their view, "proper regulation of the game [was] almost unknown." In addition, the Connecticut gaming commission was invariably chaired by political functionaries of both major political parties, whose inspectors never visited a fronton without advance warnings.

Harvey Ziskis, a Hartford fronton employee who had watched the Miami Syndicate make millions, and Lester Snyder began raising uproar about jai alai at about the same time as *Hartford Courant* investigative reporter Theodore A. Driscoll began his series on the sport in Connecticut. Public reports suggested that there had been corruption since 1976, the first year of jai alai in Hartford and Milford. Jai alai in Bridgeport, Connecticut, began in 1977 in circumstances that hardly fostered confidence.

If the original owner of Bridgeport Jai Alai could be believed, it all began with a $250 bribe to John Bailey, former national chairman of the national Democratic Party. A judge cleared Bailey's name, but rumors persisted that the Miami Syndicate members were fronting bets for "richer and more sophisticated criminals."

"It's not just at one [fronton] and it's not just at two, it's at all of them" claimed Dan Bradley, then serving as a division director of the Florida Pari-Mutuel Commission, describing similar gambling irregularities attributable to the Miami Syndicate in Florida's ten frontons.

Harvey Ziskis discovered it all, or so it seemed. He became a food concession manager at the Hartford Fronton in 1976. Not long after starting, Ziskis noticed a quartet of thirty-something fronton flies who always wore sport shirts, running shoes, and jeans filled with jai alai cash; if these clowns could make this easy money, why couldn't he?

His time was largely his own once he set up the food concessions for each evening session, so he began to watch the so-called Miami Syndicate develop their skills. He watched them avoid betting on players (or pairs of players) who, during the eight-games-per-session evenings, tended to lose rather than win.

The Syndicate players learned never to bet on players six, seven or eight, or any combination of those numbers, simply because players (or pairs) bearing those numbers very seldom won.

Using this perfectly legal system, *Hartford Courant* reporter Ted Driscoll estimated the Syndicate turned the tables on the jai alai ownership who later sold out to Roger Wheeler, earning 12 percent or more on wagers made.

The Syndicate did even better after persuading certain employees to give them critical computer reports every ninety seconds. This accommodation "allowed Syndicate members to stay away from . . . heavily played numbers," increase their earnings on each bet and eventually even finagle the size of their earnings to avoid having the IRS withhold 20 percent.

It is no surprise that Syndicate members soon became Hartford regulars. Eventually, they were assigned their own cashier and ticket puncher. Not to be outdone by a rival, the Bridgeport fronton gave Syndicate members a private lounge, television monitor and, of course, the all-important computer printouts.

Before long, Milford fronton employees threw in all of this and more, according to allegations reported by *Sports Illustrated*, whose reporters claimed that the official Milford handicapper was bribed to omit Syndicate frontons from his tout sheet, thus potentially increasing Syndicate winnings.

Some of these Hartford, Bridgeport and Milford Fronton employees earned more from the Syndicate than from World Jai Alai.

Ziskis began to develop his own system derived from what he'd seen, but his $15,000 boodle was gone within a week. Just as he was watching the Syndicate players, they were probably watching him via the computer printouts he didn't have access to and considered him competition they didn't need. He somehow raised more money and won some bets, but three nights into his winning streak at Hartford, Ziskis was accused of trying to steal a $478 winning ticket and was barred from the fronton.

Maybe he was a sore loser, but after several unsuccessful efforts, Ziskis got a gaming commission hearing on his Syndicate allegations. The commission found his allegations were unfounded, but, in a dissent, Lester B. Snyder said on the record that the commission investigation hadn't gone far enough. Snyder also wondered about the millions of dollars the Syndicate members were betting and said so.

Two of the Syndicate members whom Ziskis identified, Paul Commonas and Rodney Woods, were cleared by the commission. However, Frederick Vines, the house handicapper at Milford, confessed later that Rodney Woods had bribed him to eliminate certain players from his tout sheet, drawing bribery convictions and fines for both of them.

By August 1978, Commissioner Snyder had enough, but, after resigning, he insisted that Connecticut Governor Grasso investigate legalized gambling, citing suspicious similarities between betting patterns Commonas followed in Milford, Connecticut and Dania, Florida frontons.

Not long after this, Florida frontons began to burn under suspicious circumstances. Naturally, this meant that the paper betting records were lost. Coincidentally, the fire insurance value on the West Palm Beach fronton (never owned by Wheeler) had been doubled to $8 million a few months before it burned.[44]

By late April 1980, some twenty-two months after Wheeler had purchased World Jai Alai, eleven Connecticut bettors and players had been arrested on game-fixing charges. Five pleaded guilty. Similar charges were then pending against some of the same individuals in Florida.

Yet, World Jai Alai president Richard P. Donovan argued that "for the one scandal in jai alai there has been a whole bunch in horse racing and dog racing." The *Washington Post* quoted unidentified witnesses as testifying that players were paid up to $150 ($400 in 2013 dollars) for each game thrown while other fronton employees allegedly sold information for $200 per week, enabling certain bettors to steer their own bets to the highest paying trifectas.

When Washington, DC, considered legalization of gambling on May 6, 1980, three different firms were vying for legalized jai alai, including World Jai Alai. A 1978 report prepared for Florida gaming authorities described him as "an associate of persons believed by the law enforcement community to be organized crime figures." When the *Washington Post* asked Callahan for comment on this description, he simply replied, "That's bull."

At that time, seven companies owned frontons across the United States, but they were loosely regulated. Florida, for example, received $17 million from jai alai taxes in 1976, but its entire enforcement force consisted of two unpaid auditors using a cheap old adding machine. This probably didn't matter anyway, since all critical elements to fix games, the players, computers, handicappers and managers were controlled by management.[45]

According to two *Boston Globe* reporters, Wheeler knew what he was getting into in purchasing WJA but was lured in by the potential return on investment. He eventually had second thoughts, but was reassured by having a number of former FBI agents on his payroll at World Jai Alai, notably H. Paul Rico, a native of Belmont, Massachusetts, and Boston College graduate.[46] This, of course, was the same H. Paul Rico who allegedly reported Wheeler's day-to-day activities to the men who eventually killed Roger Wheeler in Tulsa.

Killing Roger Wheeler at Southern Hills turned out to be quite easy.

Chapter 2

In the Shadows of
Yankee Babylon

Out Ireland have we come.
Great hatred, little room,
Maimed us at the start.
I carry from my mother's womb
A fanatic heart.[1]

James Joseph "Whitey" Bulger grew up gazing at pale, distant towers that marked the boundaries of an ebbing Protestant ascendancy. Downtown Boston was bordered by mostly Catholic Poles, Lithuanians, Italians, and his own troublesome Irish. Close friends in South Boston called him Jim. "We were in a neighborhood, an enclave, [from] which a trip downtown was considered 'going to Boston,'" Whitey's younger brother William B. "Billy" Bulger, remembered. Make no mistake, the Irish of South Boston, Dorchester, Charleston, and Somerville were indeed outsiders. Even in the early twentieth century, Boston prejudice against Irish Catholics was so ingrained that entrepreneur Joseph P. Kennedy, father of the thirty-fifth president of the United States, eventually chose to do business elsewhere.

The Beginnings of Evil

New York City has, for a variety of reasons, always been the leading American metropolis of the criminal gangs. Internecine gang warfare has a long, cruel history. Back in the 1850s in New York, much of the gang rivalry and bloody fighting was concentrated around the slum known as Five Points, an area of grinding poverty. Packs of hoodlums roamed the streets, posturing and harassing the residents. The old days of fists and boots quickly changed to knives, hatchets, brass knuckles, spiked clubs, and even a tomahawk or two. Firearms were not long in coming.

The New York gangs all sported fanciful names. In addition to the better known Plug Uglies, Dead Rabbits, and Forty Thieves, there were the Kerryonions, the Shirt Tails, the Patsy Conroys, and the Chichesters, to name only a few of the early immigrant gangs. Down along the Bowery were concentrated American-born gangs such as the Bowery Boys and the True Blue Americans. Gang rivalry was not only among the gangs of Irish toughs but also with outside rivals. The gangs grew in Hell's Kitchen, too, one of them being the Gopher Gang, pronounced "Goofer" for reasons lost in the mists of history.

On top of the machismo-driven aggression common to young gangsters, there was some of the bitter Catholic-Protestant rivalry left over from the old country. It would die away slowly. The Irish took a back seat to nobody. One hoodlum put it well, and probably spoke for all or nearly all of his partners in crime: "I guess we thought we had to be crazier than everybody else, 'cause we were the Irish guys.'"[2]

The combatants were not all men, either. Women commonly handled reconnaissance and supply, but a number of them joined the ranks of the fighters. One memorable Dead Rabbit hellion rejoiced in the name of Hell-Cat Maggie. Maggie won a measure of renown by having her teeth filed to sharp points and wearing artificial fingernails, razor-sharp and pointed like stilettos.[3] She wasn't the only female terror in the gangland wars. Sadie the Goat won her name through her demonstrated expertise in head-butting opponents. She was at least as well known for a locket she wore around her neck containing one of her ears, chewed off in combat by another ferocious harridan known as Gallus Mag.[4] Mag, a woman of English origin, ran the Hole in the Wall bar, a joint the toughest American westerners would have described as a low-down dirty saloon.

Gradually, the New York gangs worked themselves into the rackets. Originally, "racket" meant nothing more sinister than a sort of public gang-run dance masquerading as a charitable enterprise. They earned much higher pay than smash-and-grab theft, rolling a drunk, or beating up a pedestrian for his wallet. Gradually, the term changed in American slang to describe any sort of organized criminal operation.

Fighting and rivalry were regular occurrences, not only in the struggle for power but also from religious anger and hatred. One example was the killing of William "Bill the Butcher" Poole, a veteran Protestant combatant and hero of the Bowery Boys. In 1854, Bill the Butcher was done in by John "Old Smoke" Morrissey, a Catholic boxing champion and Tammanyite. After a memorable hand-to-hand battle, both men emerged battered and bloody but unbowed. The fight was a draw; however, after being stabbed and shot in the heart, Poole died an astonishing fourteen days later. "Goodbye, boys," said Bill as he shuffled off this mortal coil, "I die a true American." Maybe he really believed it — or maybe not. But whoever he died as, he became a martyr for the cause. As men and women on both sides lost their fights, there was always a bit more fuel for the gangs' fire.

Some time after Bill the Butcher bit the dust, a gang called the Whyos acquired the coveted reputation as the worst gang in New York, a distinction they held at least for the last quarter of the nineteenth century. Some of the members' names were typical of gangland "handles" in the vain hope that the name would actually make them somebody: Piker, Baboon, Hoggy, Googy, and Slops.

The Irish gangs had been active in New York for four

decades before the thugs of the Italian mafia appeared. Early in the Irish immigration, Tammany Hall was the New York headquarters for organized crime, and it became an early home to many Irish hoodlums. It was a symbol of those who ran the dirty doings of New York, with a great deal of political support from city hall and the tall dogs who bossed the wards of the city. The immigrants found Tammany an already smoothly functioning criminal operation when they crossed the broad Atlantic, and they joined it with enthusiasm.

Tammany Hall had been an established criminal apparatus for about a century by the time the Irish began to join. Founded in Philadelphia and named for a mythical Indian chief called Saint Tammany, Tammany Hall had begun life as a sort of fraternal organization. It even elected its president, called the Grand Sachem, in line with the Indian term. Its function seems to have been innocent enough at first, simply the promotion of commercial welfare of its members and their friends. The honest business ambitions would change drastically.

The early gang days were a turbulent, bloody time, reaching its bloodiest day on Independence Day of 1857 with the Dead Rabbits Riot.

A long and bitter rivalry led up to the battle. The riot began when, instead of celebrating the holiday with fireworks, the Roach Guards and the Dead Rabbits marched down to the Bowery to attack the clubhouse of the Atlantic Guards and the Bowery Boys. The gang members met them on the streets, which turned the Bowery into a full-scale battlefield.

The clash had been a long time in building, the child of much animosity over the years. The gangs of New York were bitter enemies, and it was hard for anybody to stay away from taking sides—police precincts and political figures split into two factions. The Metropolitans were loyal Democrats; the Municipals were Republican. That schism produced law enforcement that was uneven at best and downright vicious. Much depended on who was getting his head busted with a nightstick and who the busters were.

The fourth of July battle went on all through the night, in and out of buildings, up and down streets. The men fought with brickbats, clubs, stones, knives, and the occasional gun. Hundreds of combatants crowded the streets. The police were strangely absent; however, they showed up in force the next morning and for once pounded the gangs without showing favoritism. The gang members were driven indoors and retreated upstairs into the tenements while the police bashed away with their clubs. One combatant fell, or was pushed, from a rooftop during the melee. He landed in the street with a fractured skull, where members of the rival gang mercilessly stomped him to death.

And so it went through the rest of the nineteenth and into the twentieth centuries. Though the fighting continued, the religious overtone was diminished. Criminal organizations gradually became a turf war, murdering for money and for control of the rackets and, especially after Prohibition, of bringing in bootlegging's astonishing profits. The conflicts themselves were more sophisticated, too. The days of breaking your opponent's head with a chunk of brick or pounding him into jelly with a piece of two-by-four were mostly gone, bloody history for the books. Some of the lads still enjoyed mayhem the old-fashioned way, but that had largely given way to powerful automobiles and deadly saltpeter.

In the early years of the twentieth century, famous New York gangster Owen "Owney" Madden started out as a prominent member of a gang called the Gophers. He was arrested a total of fifty-seven times before he was through. He managed to survive at least six bullets in his body. Madden was born in Leeds, England, in 1881, to Irish parents and did nine years of a ten-to-twenty-year sentence in Sing Sing. Madden was one of the lucky ones. He survived and eventually rose to become "duke of the west side," with partnerships in such fabled watering holes as the Cotton

Club and the Stork Club. He got involved in more gangland murder, however; had his parole revoked; and did another year of his original sentence. That convinced him it was time to retire from New York to Hot Springs, Arkansas, in the 1930s. In those days, Hot Springs was a refuge for big-city hoodlums, a crooked town where a criminal could be reasonably safe and could run his own rackets, if he wanted.

He died peacefully, but not all gang members were as lucky as Madden. Most went on to a grubby existence in their old neighborhoods, fighting bloody battles with rival gangs and dying on the street or in prison.

The Gangs of Boston

Well before the New York gangs were born, full-scale gang warfare was a Boston fixture.

In the eighteenth century, two rival mobs held a deadly tradition on Guy Fawkes Day, the anniversary of the 1605 gunpowder plot to blow up the British Parliament by a small band of Catholic conspirators. Fawkes's name was synonymous with treason and murder.

In Boston, the two gangs, called "North-End" and "South-End," built huge floats and paraded through the city streets in costume, blowing "pope horns" and demanding that householders and businesses contribute money on threat of broken windows. The gangs were both Protestant and the anti-papal fury shared, but the two opponents were not allies. Their floats carried large figures representing the devil and the Pope. Inside the structures, small boys pulled on cords to make the effigies move. The processions ended when the floats were parked and the effigies burned in huge bonfires.

This ceremony was followed by a mass battle between the two gangs, each said to be composed of some two thousand rioters. This was no pretend war. As a newspaper commented in 1745, "several were sorely wounded and bruised, some left for dead, and rendered incapable of any business for a long time."[5] This brawl seems to have been an annual festivity, augmented by any hoodlum who wanted to join in. It was fought, as an observer commented, "with clubs and cutlasses" and whatever else came to hand. Accidents occurred, too; in 1764, a boy fell under the "Pope" wagon of the North-End gang and was killed.

These annual, bloody fracases continued into the early years of the American Revolution. After the American victory, however, the atmosphere changed, since the new American republic had declared itself tolerant of all religions, and many Catholic Marylanders had joined the Continental Army. More importantly, America was now allied with Catholic France, and Gen. George Washington issued a particularly pointed and emphatic order commanding tolerance. The general's decree carried much weight.

The last remnant of the early wars in Boston seems to have been noisy processions in which the papal effigy was replaced with one representing Benedict Arnold, the hero of the French and Indian War who defected to the British. There were other cases of young Boston hoodlums invading homes in a sort of trick-or-treat of the Christmas season, although the big North-End-versus-South-End battles were now a thing of the past.

You could refer to the mobs that attacked British troops in Boston before the Revolution as gangs. The famous Boston Massacre was only one incident in a long history of anger and friction. There were plenty of criminal combines—large and small, established and spontaneous—in the days that followed the Revolutionary War. There were the rampaging street mobs of the draft riots of the 1860s, heavily comprised of Irishmen; these were so violent that troops had to be called in to settle them—even by opening fire. Then came the street hoodlums who plagued Boston in the years after the war.

As gang territory, crime, and warfare evolved, the battles became more personal. There were no rules, if there ever had been. It was a down-and-dirty struggle for prestige, money, and power, and anything was fair game. Lots of the young gang members went to jail, and in those days, jail generally was a bit tougher than just time behind bars. A trip to the jug for a gang member usually included at least one working-over by the police.

Neither beatings nor the threat of imprisonment deterred the gangs. The gang members postured, boasted, and strutted for a while, rejoicing in their illusory importance and nicknames: Punchy, the Animal, the House-Painter, the Executioner, and an assortment of Fat Tonys and a couple of Fat Vinnies—not to mention the Rifleman, also known as Steve Flemmi, Whitey's right-hand man.

The gang wars were inevitable. Turf was all important, for such underhanded activities as the gangs ran depended on having a fief, a dependent neighborhood in which and from which the gang could carry on its nefarious trade.

When the Great Migration from Ireland came, the influx of hundreds of thousands of desperate people launched the gangs as a real power on the East Coast, starting in New York. The migration was driven by widespread hardship in the old country, and some of those troubles it brought to the new land.

Hunger

We left our homes in forty-seven
Turned our backs against the wind
From our ships of creakin' timber
We bid farewell to a famished land.
   —from "Staten Island," by the Irish Rovers

Boston has had something of a genteel reputation in popular imagination. It was, after all, the scene of the formative days of the country. There is also the widespread, imperishable image of the Boston upper crust, rhyme and all:

And this is good old Boston,
The home of the bean and the cod,
Where the Lowells talk only to Cabots,
And the Cabots talk only to God.

No doubt that the verse was at least a semi-accurate picture of the aristocracy of Boston, but down in South Boston, it was a whole different world.

Most Irish immigrants had arrived in the United States with almost nothing but the clothes on their backs, driven to a new land by the great potato famine. The famine killed about one Irish citizen in seven and debilitated a great many more. Those who migrated left the dead and the weak behind. The Irish Rovers sang eloquently about that misery:

Still we hear their voices calling
On the wind we hear the sound
Friends and loved ones,
Old and young ones,
Lie beneath the famine ground.

The potato had long been the staple food of Ireland, but, in the 1800s, a virus struck and wiped out several successive years of harvests. There had been bad harvest years in the past, but this was different and much, much worse. It was no longer a question of getting through a lean year. It became a question of how to keep yourself and your children alive. Because of Irish dependence on the potato and a growing tendency over the years to plant only single variety, the virus killed a great part of the available food supply. The horror of the famine is almost beyond imagining—the anguish of mothers and fathers watching their children starve, watching famished animals gnawing on the dead, seeing three or more dead and dying people in a single bed.

Anything was better than that, even a new, foreign world somewhere on the other side of an enormous ocean.

That land across the Atlantic was as distant as the moon to the average Irish man or woman, whose world had never extended more than a few miles from home. Getting to the new land meant weeks of sailing in cramped, crowded, pitching windjammers. Still, millions of people decided it was better to sail into the vast unknown than to stay in the charnel house that was Ireland.

And so people abandoned the only homes they had ever known and left Ireland far behind to come to the land of opportunity. They went to work at anything they could get and lived anywhere they could, starting with run-down, dirty, crowded tenements, dreary places whose only virtue was the lowest possible rent. That was all that most new Irish immigrants could afford.

The Irish were at the bottom of the social ladder. The jobs they could find were mostly menial and provided a poor living. At least they could eat, but otherwise the quality of their lives was nearly as bad as it had been back in Ireland. They did not want to wait a lifetime to see some improvement in their lives and their families. Their driving need was to get ahead any way possible. It was not important that some of the most direct means to early prosperity ran through crime and crooked rackets, loan-sharking, protection, extortion, prostitution, and the like.

So were born the Irish gangs of Boston, cousins of sorts to the secret gangs of the Old Sod, the Molly Maguires, the Whiteboys, and the Ribbonmen, the product of resentment of British rule and of violence and conspiracy. Inevitably, the gangs competed for territory and bigger shares of dirty business. As with most gang rivalries, there was a great deal of posturing and big talk, but there also was potential for real cruelty and violence. Over and over, conflicts led to gang warfare.

In New York, Irish gangsters were a valuable asset if

you had need of mercenary muscle. They turned out to be natural-born political enforcers, leg-breakers of talent, and on-call killers. They became the chief warriors for Tammany Hall in New York and for politicians elsewhere on the eastern seaboard and as far west as Chicago. They were the lads who roamed the precincts on election day, working for all shades of political opinion. The Irish gangs were not much concerned with political doctrine; what mattered to them was supporting the politicians who scratched their backs in return.

The Boston Irish were unlike their New York counterparts in two primary respects. First, there was no unifying political machine similar to New York's Tammany Hall or Kansas City's Tom Pendergast machine. James Michael Curley, the most exalted of all Boston politicos, never had the citywide power that "Boss" Tweed had exercised in New York; local ward bosses in the predominately Irish "tribal villages" of South Boston, Roxbury, Dorchester, and Somerville did as they pleased, with or without Curley's permission.

As a result, four Irish tribes emerged in South Boston, in the neighborhoods of Roxbury, Dorchester, Somerville, and Charlestown. Each carried its own political independence, due in part to fragmentation and laxity in the competing Italian Mafia's North End stronghold, eventually governed by the Patriarca crime family, headquartered in Providence, Rhode Island.[6]

The gangs flourished during National Prohibition. While America was dry, the Irish gangs reached their heyday. They had arrived — they were somebody — and if they weren't universally loved, they were certainly widely feared. In their dirty business, fear produced more fruitful outcomes.

The repeal of Prohibition ended the glory days, and times became tougher for the gangs. Once the long-illegal thirst of a parched public could be lawfully slaked, it was back to the old rackets and systems.

Prohibition-Era Boston

Boston at its core is a small town . . . the strong connections which once linked Brahmin bluebloods and the literary elite are eerily mirrored by the ties among the hit men, loan sharks, guns-for-hire and dope dealers who also walked Boston's streets.[7]

When the Boston gangs first began, their biggest rivals were each other. Only later did Mafia gangsters enter the picture. The most notable early twentieth-century Irish gang in Boston was the Gustins, who took their moniker from Gustin Street in "Southie," as South Boston is known. Three brothers, Frank, Steve, and James Wallace, began in about 1910 as "tailboard thieves," or tailgaters, hijacking delivery trucks at intersections. They soon expanded into armed robbery and, with the advent of Prohibition in 1920, bootlegging. The Gustins even used counterfeit treasury-agent credentials to redirect their competitors' shipments to Gustin operations.

Of course, there were bumps along the road. Frank Wallace once was charged with robbing the *Detroit News* of $14,000. He was acquitted and spent the rest of the twenties accumulating Gustin gang power. On December 21, 1931, Frank and two of his Gustin gunsels, Barney "Dodo" Walsh and Timothy Coffey, ventured into Boston's North End. The Gustins went there to discuss a $50,000 liquor shipment that belonged to Patriarca family member Joe Lombardo. The Gustins had hijacked the alcohol a week earlier.

When Frank knocked on Lombardo's third-floor office in the Testa building in the North End, guns began barking. Wallace and Walsh were killed in the ensuing gunfight, but Coffey ran for safety into a lawyer's office. World War I veterans preparing Christmas baskets for the poor one floor above went about their tasks without hearing anything.

Without Frank's leadership, the Gustin gang waned out of power. His brother James quickly dropped out of sight. Steve Wallace was acquitted of trying to kill a police detective, tried again for the same cop, and surrendered in Boston on October 29, 1934.[8]

During Prohibition (1920-33), the sawed-off shotgun and the fully-automatic Thompson submachine gun became the weapons of choice, although pistols and rifles were regularly used, including the Browning automatic rifle ("BAR") originally produced for the military. A Thompson cost a few hundred dollars back then. You didn't need a permit, and you could even order one by mail. Almost anyone could provide Thompsons, BARs, hand grenades, and just about anything else short of a cannon.

The King of Boston

Even in the early days, neither the Irish nor the Italians had a monopoly over the Boston underworld, if the career of Charles "King" Solomon is any proof. We have a picture of him at his legendary nightclub, the Cocoanut Grove, in the heart of Boston that says a great deal about the image he wished to project. The setting was supposed to show Solomon as sophistication personified. The King and two cronies, all in elegant tuxedos, sat at a champagne-laden table gabbing with his expensively dressed "companion," Dorothy England. Pity that Solomon would be gunned down in a dank bathroom at the after-hours Cotton Club.

"You got my stash, now what do you want?" the King snapped at the Irish thugs who had him cornered in the Cotton Club bathroom, about a mile and several social classes away from his own place. Apparently, King Solomon expected some deference. Instead, he was shot four times in the chest, abdomen, and neck before staggering out onto the dance floor for some last words worthy of any gangster film actor, saying, "the dirty rats got me," or less dramatically, "the rats got me." Either way, Solomon's $4,600 wad of cash was nowhere to be found. About an hour later on January 24, 1933, Boston's greatest criminal impresario of that era was dead at age forty-seven.

Solomon was born in Russia but grew up in Salem, Massachusetts. Twenty years before his death, the police had nabbed him and Golda Solomon, most likely his relative, for maintaining a house of prostitution. Undeterred, Charles Solomon soon branched into practically every form of criminal enterprise known—except for art theft—before focusing his efforts on bootlegging, where the money was. Prohibition eventually gave Solomon ample means to purchase three Boston theaters, some New York hotels and factories, as well as Boston's once renowned Cocoanut Grove nightclub, in which almost five hundred revelers burned to death about nine years after his death.

Whether out of friendship, admiration, or simple curiosity, thousands of Bostonians lined the streets of nearby Brookline to watch his funeral procession. Eventually, three Irish gunmen with no apparent gang connections were convicted of his killing. Two did time for manslaughter and one, John F. O'Donnell, for being an accessory after the fact.

"Boston Charlie," as the King was sometimes called, might have simply been killed for the $4,600, but more conspiracy-oriented observers couldn't help but notice that Solomon had been indicted for rum running fifteen days before his death. Perhaps, those cynical souls speculated, somebody wanted the King to go under.[9]

Gradually, the Irish gangs of Boston became more and more active in all aspects of the rackets: business extortion, prostitution, loan sharking, gambling, and even gun running back into the old country, as long as it was profitable. An uneasy peace of sorts fell upon the Hub, as Boston was called, although it was sometimes interrupted by violent wars. Prostitution, gambling, and liquor markets were divided between the Italians and the Irish. Each gang had low level members of the other tribe, but, in later days, there were even a few Italian names in Irish-gang leadership.

One thing that most members of the Irish gangs had in common, Irish or not, was a loyalty to one another. Of course, this was motivated primarily by fear, but such commitment went only so far. Some would switch sides or become informers if self-interest required it. Gang historian T. J. English put it neatly: "Everything about the gangster's life is a rebuke to the mundane, everyday life of the solid citizen. He lives in the moment, pursues immediate gratification with reckless abandon and revels in his own narcissism like a slop-house pig."[10]

Much blood would stain the sidewalks of Boston before the gang feuds died away. It took a long time and left behind much heartache and enmity and a lot of corpses scattered over the sidewalks of the city. Gang warfare on the streets would never be the same again.

Chapter 3
The Politico and the Thief

James Joseph "Whitey" Bulger, who preferred to be called Jim, was born the second of six children near Boston in early September 1929, the month before the stock market crash that launched the Great Depression. He got the nickname from his shock of white-blond hair. Although he was universally known as Whitey, when people spoke to him, he was always Jim or Jimmie.

Whitey's mother, Jane Veronica McCarthy, grew up in nearby Charlestown and was twenty years younger than their father, James Joseph Bulger, for whom Whitey was named.[1] The Bulger patriarch was not many generations out of Ireland and trying to make a living for his growing family.

According to one tale that Billy, Whitey's younger brother, told, their father worked as a railroader until two freight cars collided in a train yard, sandwiching him in the middle. Canadian records, however, indicate that what really happened is far less praiseworthy. According to the documentation, Bulger the elder injured himself trying to hop a train.[2] One arm was so badly mangled that a doctor barely looked at it before he started cutting. The family of eight was condemned to poverty. Hardly anybody was rich in South Boston, "Southie" to its residents, but then, getting along there was cheap. There wasn't much work around for a one-armed man, so the family had trouble scraping by. James Bulger had a prosthetic arm fitted, but it was only marginally useful and a source of great embarrassment—he kept his wooden hand jammed into his pocket whenever he could.

After living in a succession of dreary apartments, the family settled in a new "project" in Southie, the Old Harbor Village housing project, where they rented three bedrooms for a very reasonable $29 per month. The cheap project was a paradise compared to their previous homes and was fairly peaceful in spite of the neighborhood gangs.

Hard times and tragedy may have begotten a distrust of private enterprise in the Bulgers—especially after the elder Bulger's treatment after his accident. In that community, it was far better to work for the government at some level, hence the great number of Irish cops and firefighters. A number of the Bulgers' neighbors were so employed and served as a model for how to succeed. Billy looked to the capital when he thought of the future; in Billy's eyes, the richest opportunities lay in politics. Future FBI agent John Connolly lived just down the street from the Bulgers; Joe Moakley, who later became a prominent Boston politician and Billy's mentor in the legislature, also lived in the area. Eventually, Moakley became one of the most powerful men in Washington as chairman of the Rules Committee in the US House of Representatives.

Buddy Leonard, who was about the age of Whitey's younger brother Jackie, also lived nearby. Leonard's destiny, like Connolly's, was wrapped up with Whitey's, albeit in a different way. In 1975, Whitey murdered Leonard when he became a threat to Whitey's control of the rackets. Growing up together in the old neighborhood went only so far.

The neighborhood influenced the two brothers in inherently different ways. "Billy, stay out of fights," James Joseph Bulger the elder had advised. "But if you can't avoid it, don't stand on ceremony." Unlike his older brother Whitey, Billy tried to do just that. One Sunday morning in the basement of St. Monica's Church, Billy heard his older friends Wally Clifford and Joey Quirk talking about Boston College High and Boston Latin, two high schools known for their strict academic standards. Walking through the South

Boston neighborhood, he finally decided what he had to do:

> BC High was then on St. James Street in Boston's South End, near City Hospital and the Immaculate Conception Church. I put on my Sunday suit and walked into the school without an appointment. I felt quite confident — a lifelong failing.
>
> Charles Doherty, the school registrar, happened to be at the lobby desk. I introduced myself and explained that I wanted to go to BC High, but that my family couldn't afford it and I wasn't qualified. However, I said, hurrying to get it all out before he could say anything, I would repeat the ninth grade and earn the money myself for the tuition. "So you see," I concluded, "I can handle the whole thing."
>
> He looked at me through steepled fingers for perhaps five seconds — it seemed like five hours — and then he nodded and said in the most casual of voices, "I think you can do it."[3]

"It was one of the most important events of my life," Billy recalled in his memoirs.

Billy was a compact, bulky brawler by nature, but mostly kept his fights in courtrooms and legislative halls. He habitually pointed his left index finger at anyone he spoke to, friend or foe, perhaps an affectation imitating John F. Kennedy. His spiritual mentor was the perpetually corrupt James Michael Curley.

Billy also came into great wealth at an early age when he discovered books. "From the beginning of that windfall, that unguided adventure, when I had to read with a dictionary open beside me to look up the words, I was deeply moved. I realized I had found something of the greatest value."[4]

When Billy wasn't in high school classes at Boston College, he earned money any legitimate way he could, working at a local grocery store or using family connections to get a "snow button," entitling him to work for the city after big storms. He also worked summers as a lifeguard. After his high school graduation, the same year that Whitey left the Air Force, Billy started undergraduate work at Boston

College but had to quit after his freshman year in 1953 for time in the US Army. Five years later, he used the GI bill to finish his English degree and completed law school at Boston College in 1961.

Billy was elected to the state legislature in 1961 and became a state senator ten years later. While in the legislature, he sponsored the first child-abuse laws in the state. Later, in the early 1990s, he authored Massachusetts's welfare reform law, which became the model for Federal Welfare to Work legislation. Billy Bulger admired James Michael Curley and became one of his biographers in 2009. When Billy returned from Army service, he voted for Curley and against the Democratic favorite largely for sentimental reasons, despite a direct request from South Boston political chieftain Joe Moakley. After hearing Curley give one of his last political speeches, Billy Bulger decided on his life's work: "I had no delusion that I had Curley's vocal gift. Nevertheless, I felt I could succeed in politics. I aspired to model my public service to the best of my ability, on my political idols: Roosevelt's social conscience, Truman's grit, Jack Kennedy's ability to inspire hope, [Joe] Moakley's capacity for service, large ambitions indeed."[5]

By 1978, he was president of the Massachusetts State Senate, a very powerful man indeed, a superior speaker who exerted great influence in the state's largely crooked political world. People called him the "most powerful man in Massachusetts," and they were probably right. Long-time Boston journalist Howie Carr succinctly summed up the political climate in the Massachusetts State House, when Billy started his political career in 1961:

> Nothing on the level,
> Everything is a deal.
> No deal too small.[6]

Billy eventually became a university president, but his white-haired older brother preferred bookies and larceny.

At first, Whitey worked alone. He eventually joined a minor street-corner gang called the Shamrocks. Years later, Billy recalled: "Jim's scrapes were small in those growing-up years, but in time there were enough of them to make him known to the police. Some policemen used their billy clubs more than their brains. And Jim was defiant and wouldn't give an inch. His speech was bold. He was often beaten, sometimes savagely. For a while, I thought that *all* police were vicious."[7]

Although Billy believed that his brother had a quick mind and the ability to excel academically, "I had seen him change from a blithe spirit to a rebel whose cause I could never discern. He was in a constant state of revolt again . . . I'm not sure what. He was as restless as a claustrophobic in a closet."

Whitey Bulger was intelligent and capable of exuding much charm when it suited him. He was always in trouble growing up, a constant truant from his school, a petty criminal from as early as when he was fourteen. He was already a tough street kid before he was even into his teens, and it got worse from there, when he joined the Shamrocks.

While in the Shamrocks, Whitey met a future FBI agent who would shelter him from the law twenty-seven years later, if not before: John Connolly, better known in Southie as "Zip." In 1948, eight-year-old Connolly and several pals wandered into a corner drugstore. While they eyed the candy counter, Whitey Bulger came into the store and offered to buy them all ice cream, but Connolly held back, thanks to the age-old parental warning not to take sweets from strangers. Whitey sensed this. "Hey kid, I'm no stranger," he said. "Your mother and father are from Ireland," Whitey reassured Connolly. "My mother and father are from Ireland. I'm no stranger. What kind of ice cream do you want?"[8] Connolly chose vanilla. A few months later, he was equally grateful when Whitey saved him from being beaten up by older kids near the Old Harbor tenements where the Connolly and Bulger families lived.

After some time at Bradford High, a trade school in Boston,

and the Air Force, from which he was honorably discharged in 1952 — despite a spotty conduct record — Whitey took a federal fall for hijacking and armed robbery. During a nine-year sojourn through three federal prisons, he became the lifelong friend of the "Choctaw Kid," Clarence Carnes, the pride of Daisy, Oklahoma, and youngest inmate ever sent to Alcatraz. Whitey was released in 1965.

The Merry Lads of Boston

The fair city of Boston had become a hub of organized crime well before the Bulgers came along. During Whitey's youth, the Italians were concentrated in the North End. The Irish gangs were found in a blue-collar district northwest of Boston called Somerville, especially in an area known as Winter Hill. There was also a considerable gang presence just north of Boston in Charlestown as well as in South Boston.

The Irish gangs hatched their plans, recruited new members, stashed and fenced their loot, partied, and bragged in their South Boston and Charlestown strongholds. Generally, they headquartered in pubs, just like the IRA and secret societies had back in Ireland. Later, they would gravitate toward garages, places where they could plot without being overheard and where they could store weapons, booty, and contraband.

At times they fought, in their own neighborhoods and elsewhere. Afterwards, they hid inconvenient corpses, permanently and without a trace. Often, however, bodies ended up lying in puddles of blood on the streets.

Growing Up a Gangster

The six Bulger children who survived to adulthood grew up in the atmosphere and subsequently learned to fend for themselves early on. Although Billy was particularly industrious, working after school at whatever he could get, with Whitey, it was different.

Whitey, the street kid, was away from home as often as he could be, doing his apprenticeship in crime. What he learned by experience would take him a long way. Young Whitey frequently got into trouble. He was thirteen when he was first arrested for larceny. Arrests for assault and battery soon followed. Whitey was equally as enterprising as Billy, but in his own way. According to a single source that has never been corroborated, he supposedly hired out as a gay prostitute, often working the patrons of a bar called Mario's Sail Aweigh.

There is a yarn first told by Whitey's enemies that in 1965, Whitey was one of the partners of singer Sal Mineo, at least briefly. The story goes that somebody barged into the green room of a joint called Blinstrub's, run by Hank Garrity. Garrity had visited Whitey while he was in Leavenworth Penitentiary.[9] It is said that when the unexpected intruder entered the room above Blinstrub's, he found Whitey and Garrity engaged in a bizarre ménage a trois entanglement with Mineo. Whitey had his picture taken in a sort of macho, bare-chested stance that would have made anybody wonder what his sexual tastes might have been.[10]

It's only fair to add that Whitey always seemed to have at least one woman *du jour,* and at least one of Whitey's old associates denies his gay involvement saying, "he had more women than Hugh Hefner." This Bulger associate attributed the range of rumors to "media malice," and both of his long-time girlfriends have called the accusations ridiculous.[11]

In any case, Whitey grew up working at his chosen profession of law breaker, first spending some time at two-bit truck "tailgating," stealing part of the cargo from a parked truck while a gang member followed the truck driver inside at each delivery stop. From there, it was but a short step to hijacking a whole truckload—a crime in which the driver was almost always complicit. Even that was small time, bush-league stuff. Whitey intended to rise in the hierarchy of the criminal world — he was interested in bigger things.

Whitey joined the Air Force in 1948, was arrested for off-duty misconduct in Great Falls, Montana, and spent some time in the stockade. Along the way, he was counseled by one of his superior officers, who tried to warn him that he was headed for a dishonorable discharge, emphasizing the effect that would have on possible employment. Whitey's answer was a look into his soul: "I could go back to the work I used to do, no matter what kind of discharge I get."[12]

Whitey received an honorable discharge on August 16, 1952, in spite of his lousy record, and did exactly what he said he could do. He picked up where he'd left off in Southie with anything crooked he could find, but inevitably his ambition led him to more serious criminal enterprises.

Whitey tried bank robbery, which ranked as the very zenith of the larceny trade. He was twenty-five, and, in his own eyes at least, was ready for the big leagues. Whitey signed on with one Carl G. Smith Jr., a professional burglar who had become an accomplished jailhouse lawyer. Smith had filed briefs that won reversal of three convictions on procedural grounds. Smith, Bulger, and other first timers robbed a Pawtucket, Rhode Island, bank in May 1955, grabbing a respectable $42,000 boodle. On this, his first bank job, Whitey held a pistol on bank personnel and customers while the rest of the crew swept up the money. Whitey's share of the loot was about $14,000, big money for a newcomer to the robbery trade. That heady success must have fueled the need for more.

The next target was a bank in Hammond, Indiana, which Whitey planned with Richard Barchard five months later. When they first scouted the targeted bank, a police officer was inside, so the gang identified a second bank in Hammond to rob at a later date. Back in Massachusetts,

Whitey and a partner robbed a bank in Melrose on November 18, 1955. About a week later in Hammond, the day before Thanksgiving, Barchard jumped over the counter at the Woodmar branch of the Hoosier State Bank and scooped up money from the tellers' cages. While Barchard gathered in the loot, Whitey kept everybody covered, this time with two handguns. The take was much smaller, but the ultimate penalty was huge.

In addition to at least three federal offenses, which virtually guaranteed an FBI manhunt, Bulger and Barchard sported identical shirts and hunting caps but no masks. Whitey dyed his hair black and began wearing horn-rimmed glasses he didn't need. He was back in Boston by Christmas, but fled to California on January 4, 1956, when a warrant was issued for his arrest. Three months later, Boston-area FBI agent H. Paul Rico learned that Whitey was back in his hometown and spending time at a particular watering hole. On the third night of the police stakeout, March 4, 1956, Whitey appeared unarmed, and the arrest went down without incident.

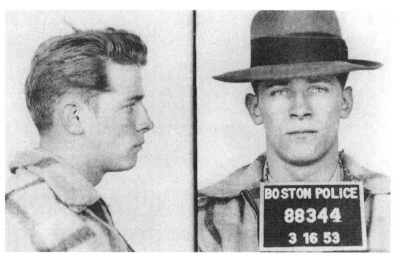

Bulger, sulky, at age twenty-three. (Courtesy Boston Police)

His family spent their meager savings on a politically connected lawyer, but Whitey was sent to the federal prison in Atlanta on a twenty-year sentence in 1956. Then, in 1959, he was sent to Alcatraz, an old-fashioned prison without opportunities for self-improvement. He was caught holding "some sort of contraband," according to brother Billy.[13]

Even though Alcatraz was the federal dumping ground for the worst scum of the criminal world, Whitey thought his stint at Atlanta had been worse. In Atlanta, he had accepted a chance to reduce his time by volunteering for experiments to test the effects of LSD. An offer like that was hard to refuse, especially for a prisoner facing as much time as Whitey was. According to his diaries, he had experienced horrors as a result. "I fear sleep," he wrote, ". . . I'm woken by a scream, and find it's me screaming."[14] In addition to terrible dreams, Whitey also recorded in his diaries a nameless fear that permeated his daily life. At the same time, he also said that he felt that by participating in the test he was "giving something back to society."[15]

Years later, Whitey learned in detail about the effects of this experiment from John Marks's 1979 book, *The Search for the Manchurian Candidate.* An informal memoir that Bulger left in a girlfriend's home was seized and published by the FBI. The memoir recounted that a Boston-area psychiatrist who administered a battery of brain-wave tests opined that Bulger had been physically damaged by the LSD experiment. Perhaps so, but nevertheless, Bulger spent a lifetime inflicting pain on society.

Whatever his reasons for participating in the LSD program, his sentence was reduced. Whitey was later moved to Lewisburg, Pennsylvania, and was released in 1965. Southie beckoned and Whitey went home, attracted by the rich prospects for another career in crime. He would be more careful this time around.

The First Irish Mob War

While Whitey was in prison, much had changed in Southie. The First Irish Gang War began on Labor Day 1961 between the McLaughlin brothers of Charlestown and Buddy McLean's crew down in Southie, eventually known as the Winter Hill gang. Before the smoke blew away, some forty gangsters were dead and scores more wounded or on the run.

One version of that conflict began when McLaughlin gang luminary Georgie McLaughlin made a not-so-subtle pass at the girlfriend of Winter Hill gang associate Alexander Petricone Jr. by pinching her monumental breasts. The lady wanted no part of it, but McLaughlin kept pushing until Petricone took umbrage and raised lumps all over Georgie. The Winter Hill boys dumped him, battered, bleeding, and unconscious, near a hospital emergency room. His worst injury was a broken nose, neither a lasting nor permanent injury. The incident should have been a tempest in a teapot, for, as Howie Winter later said "a broken nose and a lady's

Winter Hill in the 1960s.

breasts" were not much of a reason for real concern.[16] The McLaughlin brothers were furious and demanded the surrender of the Winter Hill man who had reduced their youngest brother to a jelly. McLean, of course, refused, on the reasonable ground that their brother plainly had it coming. This loosed the dogs of war in Charlestown and Somerville.

Before this incident, the McLaughlins and McLeans had avoided violence, at least against each other. Bernard "Bernie" and Edward "Punchy" McLaughlin were primarily minor loan sharks to ordinary citizens. Punchy McLaughlin's droopy-eyed, coarse country looks and grim stare starkly contrasted with James L. "Buddy" McLean, a clean-cut all-American charismatic kid to whom people naturally gravitated. Repayment was by installment, and the profit was in the "vig:" interest of 5 percent and up, usually much higher. "Vig" was said to be a Russian word for "winnings;" in English, however, it translated into illegally exorbitant interest charges.

The beauty of the McLaughlins' local loan-sharking business was that there were very few bad debts. If somebody didn't pay, or didn't pay on time, you sent one or two goons to "reason" with the debtor, either with fists, a baseball bat, or even an ice pick in the eye. If you didn't get all your money from that borrower, at least the word got around that it didn't pay to be late.

Buddy McLean was one of a kind—a handsome, smart, ambitious kid who'd done a hitch in the Marines and then worked his way to respectable prosperity, often working two jobs at once. His day job found him along the water as a longshoreman. Only in his early twenties did he become a partner in his own trucking business, which led to a loan-sharking racket as well.

Buddy was a famous brawler, having built a reputation for fighting anybody at the drop of a hat. Married, with four kids, and working brutal hours, he still found time to call in at Joe Donahue's Capital Bar, a fixture in Winter Hill. He did enough fighting there that Donahue told him, "Buddy, you keep tossing guys against the wall, I ain't gonna have a bar left."[17]

The spark that most likely ignited the feud went far beyond women, resentment, and threats. It was an attempt by some McLaughlins, probably including Whitey's future partner Stevie Flemmi, to wire a bomb beneath McLean's car. They weren't very adept, since they left at least one dangling wire visible. A neighbor spotted it and warned McLean.

Not only did the bomb not work, but the car they had chosen to blow up was transport for McLean's family. A man's family was off limits, even if he was an enemy. To make matters worse, McLean's wife had intended to use the car that day. Buddy McLean was looking for blood.

He got it the old-fashioned way the next day. McLean shot Bernie McLaughlin in the back of the head at high noon on Halloween of 1961 in Charlestown Square in front of a number of witnesses, none of whom could identify the shooter clearly. There is a tale that after Bernie hit the pavement, a man stood over him and said, "Bernie, you poor bastard, you're dying and the guy who did this should get a medal."[18]

What followed Bernie's murder was full-scale war. Everybody was in the line of fire, and blood covered Charlestown and Somerville before the smoke finally blew away.

War to the Knife

There was no certainty about the loyalties of many Somerville men, especially if they were not firmly attached to one side or the other. Men who ordinarily would remain neutral could be pressured, and as a result, they were dangerous. Buddy devised a system he called "preventive maintenance" in which men called "clockers" followed uncommitted men who might have yielded to pressure. Every movement of a possible defector was recorded, however innocent. After a reasonable period of time, the clocker handed the subject a piece of paper crammed with a detailed history of his movements. There were no threats, no violence — the record was generally enough to deprive the other side of a potential ally.[19]

The McLaughlins repeated their attempt to blow up Buddy McLean in 1962, and once again they failed. They fouled up the firing device so that Buddy drove around for a whole day un-dynamited. When the bomb finally blew, he wasn't in the car at all. They tried once more, this time the traditional way, using a criminal. Ron Dermody was a short kid with tall, thick, swept-back hair who was wildly enamored of Dorchester Dottie, the former wife of Whitey's bank-robbing partner Richard Barchard. He agreed to murder Buddy in September 1964 in return for the murder of Spike O'Toole, Dottie's current flame, which, he thought, would clear the way for his own carnal desires.

Dermody was as good as his word, filling his quarry with bullets — only it was the wrong man, a petty thief named Charlie Robinson unconnected with the war. Dermody ended up dead in his small, white Fiat on September 4, 1964, his glasses knocked to the car floor.[20]

Dottie, however, wasn't too innocent herself. She set up a particularly nasty strike against Harold Hannon and Wilfred Delaney, a pair of McLaughlin partisans, earlier that year in August. While entertaining them, she excused herself to "run an errand." A couple of McLean gunmen arrived after her departure, and the McLaughlin men departed Dottie's place in a rolled-up rug stuffed into a trunk. They were fished out of Boston Harbor on August 20, 1964.[21]

Buddy McLean managed to survive a long time, in spite of a paucity of grey matter — take his experiment with his .38, for example. He had heard that the potato was an effective explosion muffler, so he decided to give it a go. The shot he fired was not muted in the slightest, and Buddy was covered with a slimy gunk of the vegetable's remains. On repeating the experiment, he achieved the same unsatisfactory result. "F--- it," he said at last. "Let's go get a drink."[22]

Meanwhile, after Bernie passed on Halloween 1961, Punchy McLaughlin rose to head the McLaughlin faction. Punchy did not enjoy his leadership position without interference for long. While waiting for another hoodlum, he was approached by what appeared to be a pair of Hasidic rabbis. He saw the shotgun too late, for the rabbis were in fact two Catholic boys, Stevie Flemmi and Frank Salemme. Punchy was lucky and got out with a torn-up jaw, but he later was shot to death waiting for a bus on October 20, 1965.[23]

Buddy McLean was not one of nature's intellectual giants, but he was long on courage, and it got him killed in the end. On October 31, 1965, eleven days after Punchy's death, he was ambushed outside a dive called Pal Joey's and died in the street, trying to pull one of his bodyguards to safety behind a car. It was four years to the day since McLean had killed Bernie McLaughlin.

Buddy was dead, but the First Irish Gang War continued until his two killers, brothers Connie and Stephen Hughes, were killed. Connie died on May 25, 1966, and Stephen followed on September 23 of the same year. Altogether, some sixty gangsters and hangers-on died during the First Irish Mob War.

The Second Irish Mob War

Some of the police were equally weak reeds as politicians. One hoodlum testified to a couple of policemen watching a killing by gang hitman "Jimmy the Bear" Flemmi. Far from arresting Jimmy the Bear, the man said that once the killer had left the scene, the policemen arranged to have the car in which the murder took place pushed into another police division so that they wouldn't have to investigate the killing. They settled for a $2,500 payoff from Jimmie's brother, Steve Flemmi. Silence, to some of the Boston police, was apparently golden in more than one way.

In Boston, the path to criminal riches was sometimes helped by official corruption that went far beyond Boston's finest. FBI agent H. Paul Rico began using Steve Flemmi as an informant in 1965. Managing the Bureau's snitches in supposed accordance with strict written FBI guidelines was the road to recognition and promotion. But in order to keep the information pipeline flowing, unscrupulous agents would ignore those guidelines. So it was with Rico, according to some law enforcement authorities.

Three years later, when another hoodlum implicated Flemmi and the equally lethal Frank Salemme in several murders, including the bombing of a lawyer's car and the deaths of several one-time gangster friends, Rico warned them that indictments were on the way. The two gangsters left Boston before the law could find them.

By then, Whitey Bulger had become a leading hatchet man for the Killeen faction in the war to control Southie. Whitey wanted more and would go on working until he got it.

Up at the capitol, Billy continued to rise. He was not, however, a complete opposite of his openly criminal brother, even on the surface. Billy was not above vitriolic oratory. He often used the old elite of Boston as his whipping boy, not sparing those Irishmen who had risen peacefully and honestly to positions of power and respect.

It was the old technique of "It's their fault!," and Billy Bulger was a master at it. He characterized his targets as, among other things, "drowning in a sea of hypocrisy," but he practiced a little of that himself, avoiding his brother in public to keep up the appearance of respectability. The extent of his back-door assistance to his brother, however, is still a matter of inquiry and speculation.

Once an unscrupulous man got himself elected, there were all manner of opportunities for self-enrichment. Of forty legislators in Billy's "entering class," five went to prison. Early in 1968, Billy, his law partner Tom Finnerty, and several political figures bought fourteen acres of "surplus" land from the United States. They paid a trifle more than $200,000, and, after a series of paper conveyances, sold it a couple of years later for nearly half a million. The future in politics, and its related opportunities, was starting to look quite promising.

The most vicious gang war of modern Boston started in 1971, the same year that Billy Bulger began hosting an annual St. Patrick's day breakfast that would eventually draw every major politico in Massachusetts. The war began when Kenny Killeen, whose brother Donald was the leading light of the dominant, highly organized Killeen gang, got into a brawl with Mickey Dwyer, a member of the smaller, less lethal Mullen gang, named for Mullen Square, the gang's former stomping ground.

Kenny ended the scrap by biting off Mickey Dwyer's nose and shooting him in the shoulder three times. Such encounters were certainly not unknown in Southie, but as this one involved men of two rival gangs, it had consequences far beyond the wrecking of Dwyer's large, upturned snout.

Donald Killeen rescued the nose from the gutter, put it in a Styrofoam chest over ice, and had it delivered to the hospital where the rest of Dwyer had been moved. The remains of the nose were sewn back on.

Despite this gesture of goodwill, the Mullen men could not let the incident pass without response, even though they were far less powerful and less organized than the Killeens.

Whitey Bulger had joined the ranks of Killeen muscle, but he was a little different from most street-gang soldiers.

Like them, Whitey killed, beat, and mutilated on order, but, according to the published memoirs of Patrick Nee, a dedicated Mullen warrior and an enemy of long standing, Whitey got a thrill out of hurting and killing other people.

In any event, despite Donald Killeen's efforts, the War of Dwyer's Nose was on. One of the casualties was Billy O'Sullivan, a skinny man called "Billy O" in Southie and a veteran Killeen soldier. Billy O had drawn first blood in February 1971 in a bar by shooting a Mullen partisan named Buddy Roache, crippling him permanently.[24]

In close support of Billy O, and maybe even his leader, was the omnipresent Whitey Bulger. The two of them most likely shot the next casualty, a man named McGonagle. They were after one of the leaders of the Mullen gang, Paulie McGonagle, but they blew the assignment. Bulger drove up beside Paulie McGonagle in broad daylight and drilled him through the head through the car window. It seemed to be clean, a perfect strike, a professional killer's dream. The shooting eliminated McGonagle permanently, except that Whitey got the wrong McGonagle. The dead man was Paulie's lookalike brother Donald, who was not even part of the gang and had taken no part in the war.

There is a story that after the bungled assassination, O'Sullivan and Whitey drove to O'Sullivan's house. "I shot the wrong one," Whitey said, as Billy began cooking. "I shot Donald." Billy's response was classic Southie: "Don't worry about it. He wasn't healthy anyway. He smoked. He would have gotten lung cancer. How do you want your pork chops?"[25]

There were other clashes, narrow escapes, killings, and woundings. One Mullen was caught in a Killeen ambush and had his left arm blown into a shattered, oozing mess. Bulger was right in the middle of it all. Twice he tried to kill Mullen member Patrick Nee, and twice he failed. Nee tried to take out Bulger once, but he missed, too.

Then the dead McGonagle's brother Paulie, a real

gangster, ambushed Billy O on March 28, 1971. The story goes that Paulie, dressed ninja style in black clothing, hid in some shrubbery for several hours waiting until his half-drunk quarry appeared. In the last few seconds of his life, Billy heard the sound of a pistol being cocked. He turned to find Paulie emerging from his bushy hiding place:

"Shit," said Billy, "I'm dead."

"You're right," said Paulie, or so Patrick Nee later told the tale.

Billy's death increased the tension and anger, and the war was just beginning. The death toll mounted until, at last, Donald Killeen went out the same way others had. At about 9:00 p.m. on May 13, 1972, Killeen decided to go out and buy a paper after hosting a birthday party for his four-year-old son, Greg. Several men converged on him as he got into his car in the darkness. One rammed a submachine gun through the window and blazed away. Killeen was hit eight times at point-blank range. He had seen the assassins coming at the last moment and reached for the .38 in his glove compartment, but he wasn't quick enough.

Whitey sent flowers collect to the funeral with a simple note that read "au revoir." Then, Whitey said his final amen to the war when he stopped his car next to Kenneth, the last surviving Killeen brother, as he was walking down the street. "You're out," he told Kenneth, "no more warnings."[26]

With Donald Killeen's death, a sort of uneasy peace came to Southie. With the leadership of the Killeens dead — or at least abruptly retired — the remaining hitters went to ground. That included Whitey Bulger, who was now being very careful with his skin.

When it appeared his side might be losing the war, Whitey made his move. According to most accounts, when Donald Killeen was killed May 13, 1972, Whitey approached Howie Winter to make a deal. Winter was the leader of the mostly Irish but commendably diverse Winter Hill gang, named for a blue-collar section of Somerville, a Boston suburb ten miles north of South Boston. Winter's last name was simply a coincidence. Howie Winter was a smart, effective leader, who not only knew how to manage a criminal enterprise as a business but also took care of his people and his neighbors, inspiring strong and lasting loyalties. For example, when a telephone company employee named Leahy was killed in an auto accident, Howie showed up almost immediately at his home with groceries although Leahy was not a gang member.

So, it seems, when Donald Killeen was killed, Whitey turned his coat, as he would again in the future. When the going got tough in the war, it is not surprising that Whitey and the other remnants of the old Killeen gang turned to Howie Winter. He was tough and able, and you could trust him, a rare quality in the dirty world of the Irish gangs.

Howie Winter and the New England Mafia, represented by the Patriarca crime family, soon mediated a peculiar merger of the surviving Mullens and Killeens into the Winter Hill gang. After all, warfare was bad for business.

Whitey's Road to Power

Although the 1972 peace agreement was brokered by Howie Winter, it was instigated by Whitey Bulger, who considered his odds of survival short without such an arrangement. The situation, which had looked like an absolute disaster for the remainder of the Killeen faction, turned into an agreement that divided Boston into racketeering territories. Suddenly bitter enemies, Whitey Bulger and Patrick Nee were Winter Hill associates.[27] Whitey had landed on his feet again; he would continue his rise under the new organization. He could, as Howie Winter plainly put it, teach the devil tricks.

For a while, Howie Winter competently guided the Winter Hill gang along the path to riches. There were various threats and rivals to Winter, which were dealt with in the customary way. One such rival was Spike O'Toole, a long-time warrior of the McLaughlin gang who spent most of his spare time at the Bulldog Tavern in a Dorchester neighborhood called Savin Hill. Whether O'Toole knew it or not, ex-pug Eddie Connors, the owner of the bar, was a buddy of Howie Winter.

When O'Toole tied one on Saturday, December 1, 1973, Eddie Connors made a phone call. John Martorano and Whitey Bulger were waiting in a car parked outside. Martorano sprayed O'Toole with a submachine gun, hitting him ten times or more, whereof he speedily departed this earth.[28] The next target was Paulie McGonagle in November 1974; Whitey took this one on himself. McGonagle was buried at Tenean Beach in Dorchester, a favorite burying ground for Whitey's victims. McGonagle's car was pushed off a pier and his wallet thrown in the water. Whitey called this sort of arranged disappearance "doing a Houdini."

According to one source, Eddie Connors started bragging about how he helped set up O'Toole. Whitey didn't like that kind of publicity, so on June 12, 1975, Howie Winter called Connors and told him to get to a secure phone booth at a particular hour. Whitey, Steve Flemmi, and Johnny Martorano turned the phone booth red without getting out of their stolen car.

During the fall of 1974, Whitey lost his only child, a son he had with Lindsey Cyr, a legal secretary and sometime model. Their son, Douglas, had inherited Whitey's intensity and sense of purpose, but he died of Reye's syndrome at age six that October. Cyr later said that she never saw Whitey laugh again.

Of Whitey, notoriously on the wrong side of the law, Billy would say only that he was a good brother and that he loved his mother; Billy piously added, "I worry for him." He had good reason, and part of that worry may have been about Billy himself. John Connolly remained a good friend of both Bulgers. Connolly often worked in Billy's election campaigns and brought new FBI agents by Billy's office. Billy later denied he knew that Connolly and Whitey had a "special relationship," but he did tell the interviewer that he'd told Connolly, "I expected him to take care of my brother."[29]

Billy hadn't abandoned Whitey at all. He was a powerful man, and it didn't pay to cross him. Witness the story of a very good state trooper, who stopped Whitey at Logan Airport in 1987 with a bag containing some $50,000.

Whitey went free, but the trooper was pursued by bureaucracy in spite of his Vietnam service, spotless police records, and service awards. In the end, he was forced into early retirement; several years later, broke and never recovered from the destruction of his world in law enforcement, he shot himself. One of Billy's political allies asked for a "copy of the report" on the airport incident, hardly the sort of thing in which a leading legislator would ordinarily have an interest. The persecution of the police officer followed.

It was reminiscent of another incident back in 1981, which followed a state police investigation into Whitey's criminal doings. It included placing a bug in the garage he used as his headquarters. The effort came to naught because Connolly tipped off Whitey about the device.

The following year, an odd clause appeared in the state's annual budget legislation. It required police officers over fifty—hardly a species of antique—to retire or face a reduction in both rank and pay. Only five officers were affected by the new provision, but three of them had been part of the attempt to nail Whitey Bulger.

Fat Tony's Big Mistake

Fat Tony Ciulla was an ace horse-race fixer who did deals with the Winter Hill gang. He decided to branch into swindling, targeting a wealthy Boston-area dentist with more money than sense. At Fat Tony's prompting, an intermediary named James Sousa convinced the dentist that he could make thousands buying a box supposedly filled with gold bars. When the dentist arrived at the scene of the switch with his ten year old son, he noticed two Winter Hill types with guns drawn. He pulled his own pistol and watched helplessly as Fat Tony grabbed his son.

The gangsters escaped, the ten-year old was released just around the corner, but Fat Tony had a potential kidnapping charge over his head. Worse still, Sousa panicked and began to ask for attorney money. He was lured to the Winter Hill hideout at the Marshall Motors garage. There, in October 1974, Martorano shot Sousa in the head and had two gang stalwarts hide the body in Boxford, Massachusetts, where he supposedly remains to this day.[30]

Sousa was hardly the last small timer to run afoul of Whitey Bulger in the mid-1970s. Richard Castucci, a middle-aged Revere, Massachusetts, hustler found himself acting as a go-between for the Hill in dealings with New York bookmaker Jack Mace. Winter Hill owed Mace $150,000 in lost football wagers in early December 1976. Later that month, Castucci ran into a problem by the name of John "Zip" Connolly, who informed Bulger that Castucci had told the FBI where Winter Hill soldier Joe McDonald could be found in New York City. Castucci, like Sousa before him, was lured to Marshall Motors in Somerville to pick up part of the $150,000 that Winter Hill owed to Mace. Martorano shot him in the head.[31]

Indian Wars

In the early 1970s, "Indian Joe" Notarangeli, who was not in fact an Indian, tried to compete with the Winter Hill gang for control of gambling in the North End. One of the early casualties was Michael Milano, an unaffiliated bartender. Johnny Martorano had gunned down Milano one dark night at a Brighton, Massachusetts, stoplight in March 1973, having mistaken Milano's red Mercedes for a brown one owned by Indian Joe. After the mistake, the Winter Hill gang threw a fundraiser for another man in the car who had been paralyzed for life from the gunfire.[32]

Whitey started the Indian Joe campaign by killing Indian Joe's associate Al Plummer with an Uzi submachine gun on March 19, 1973. Destroy Plummer he did, very nearly blowing his head off and incidentally wounding two other men in the car where Plummer sat.

The murderous John Martorano got still another of Indian Joe's people, a man named O'Brien, ventilating him seventeen times with a submachine gun on March 27, 1973, while Whitey drove the hit car. In April, Martorano posed as a construction worker — complete with yellow hard hat — walked into a coffee shop, and calmly shot Indian Joe twice. Nobody saw a thing.

Less than a year later, on February 21, 1974, Indian Al, Joe's brother, went out on the dirty end of a Martorano bullet. A short time later, the police stopped some joyriding teenagers in Somerville and discovered Indian Al in the trunk of their stolen car.

Soon thereafter, Whitey began working regularly with Steve Flemmi, nicknamed "The Rifleman." Flemmi had meritorious Korean War service, in which, according to his own account, he saw action against both North Korean and Chinese infantry. "Stevie" Flemmi, the product of a marriage between Italian immigrants, was just as evil as Bulger.

Flemmi had a brother, Vincent, who was equally lethal. All he wanted to do, according to one FBI report, was "to kill people . . ."[33] Similarly, hitman Joe Barboza, called "Joe the Bear," a child of Portuguese immigrants and a Sicilian wannabe, became a local legend when he killed one gangster and then removed his head.

"The Rifleman."

The 1977 Pinball Wars

Although Indian Joe and his boys were now out of the picture, Howie Winter soon got into a conflict over the profitable pinball racket in Somerville. There was a great deal of money to be made in pinball, but the "rentals" the gangsters attached to their pinball machines put them at a competitive disadvantage with honest vendors. Winter's solution was a vintage mob tactic; he threatened any competitor who violated the Winter Hill gang monopoly.

One such honest competitor went to the local district attorney. In late 1977, Winter and Sal Sperlinga were pinched. Winter was convicted of extortion and later on horse-race fixing charges. When Howie Winter went to prison in 1979, Whitey became the real king of Winter Hill.

Despite a declared moratorium on violence beginning in 1973, Whitey and his associates killed a number of old Mullen rivals now operating within the newly merged Winter Hill gang, notably Paulie McGonagle, the rival Whitey had tried to kill two years earlier when he killed poor Donald McGonagle by mistake.

The next year, in 1980, Whitey began regularly teaming up with Stephen "The Rifleman" Flemmi. Whitey probably didn't learn that Flemmi was a rat under the tutelage of FBI Special Agent H. Paul Rico until 1981, when the FBI recruited him, too.

It had been a tough road, but he had finally arrived at the top of his chosen heap. Whether this was the first time he wore it or not, Whitey blossomed out with a large showy belt buckle inscribed "ALCATRAZ, 1934-1963."

In his chosen business, he wasn't afraid to advertise.

A Guardian Angel

If there was a good guy in the tangled world of Boston

An angry Bulger in Alcatraz. (Courtesy Federal Bureau of Prisons)

criminal politics it was big Sal Sperlinga. Yes, nearly everybody agreed, he had a felony conviction, but his crusade to keep Somerville safe for its residents won him widespread respect and affection.

Sal, an ex-Marine who had served in World War II, was a bookie by trade. He was a friend to Howie Winter and largely insured the peace in Somerville in the late 1970s, in partnership with Howie. Buddy McLean was long gone, and so were his Charlestown murderers from the McLaughlin gang. There were a few independent bookies in the area, mostly older men not affiliated with the Winter Hill mob, but as Howie put it, "we really were 'live and let live' guys." Coexistence was the order of the day.

That did not sit well with some of their constituents, men such as Whitey Bulger and Steve Flemmi, who thought that all these outsiders should be closed down, by force if necessary. Howie and Sal weren't having any of it, as Bulger and Flemmi were only small-time gangsters at that time, men whose opinions counted for very little.

Take the attempt by two North End loan sharks to move in on a local doughnut shop, claiming the owner's son owed them money. Sal intervened: "I think you should tell this woman you're very sorry for scaring her family . . . you never should have let the kid get in that deep . . . Next time you have customers from Somerville, you come and see me."[34] That was the last anybody heard of the North Enders. Sal had that effect on people, for his reputation preceded him. For a while, he was successful in keeping the outsiders away. But then he made a big mistake.

Sal had confronted a drug dealer named Daniel Moran, a specialist in angel dust and heroin. When he told Moran to stop, the gangster shot his mouth off and Sal whipped him in return. The pusher took his revenge, shooting down the unarmed Sperlinga in a private social club on January 4, 1980. Moran went to jail for life, but Sal was gone.

Chapter 4
A Classic Entrepreneur

He was a classic entrepreneur — tenacious and aggressive — who drove himself and others to the limit in building an eclectic business empire. . . .[1]

Sankaty Head, near the village of Siasconset, Massachusetts, was never the same once Roger Wheeler built his forty-five-hundred-square-foot house among the long-established residences of Nantucket Island nobility. The island was a three-hour ferry ride from Cape Cod and a world away from Whitey Bulger's South Boston empire.

Wheeler had some trees in front of the house removed on one cold winter's night because they blocked his view. This prompted a Siasconset tour guide to turn up the speakers on his trolley every time he passed the house and yell insults about the "Rich Okie" into his microphone.[2]

Wheeler couldn't care less. It was 1978, and he was absorbed in the deal of a lifetime — or so he thought. The business opportunity had a cash-generating potential far beyond the first deal he had made two decades earlier. His fax machine was churning out thick proposals and counterproposals from World Jai Alai, a sports-betting operation in Miami.

Even today, some thirty years after his death, litigation-prone Roger Milton Wheeler is considered a Tulsa business colossus. Stories of his rise from salesman to top-shelf executive, accounts of hallway firings, and urban legends of altered contracts and recollections of bluffs are still told in places where the Tulsa business community gathers.

May 1978. Roger Wheeler is one of the first American tourists allowed to enter China. (Courtesy Wheeler Family)

Although Wheeler had made most of his fortune in Tulsa, he wasn't an Okie at all. Born on February 27, 1926, in Boston, three years before Whitey Bulger, he grew up about fourteen miles from South Boston in Reading, Massachusetts. His childhood home was a modest Victorian on High Street. Roger had never traveled to posh Nantucket Island as a kid, but he had heard all about it when he and his brother Albert had worked in Cape Cod restaurants during summer breaks as teenagers. So, when he was rich enough, he built his own home on the prestigious Nantucket Island.

Wheeler came from modest yet more affluent circumstances than Bulger. His maternal grandfather was a native of Canada, who had become an American citizen at age twenty-two. Sidney Sea Wheeler, Roger's father, a Chicago native with Kentucky ancestry, was a printer for the *Christian Scientist Monitor* for more than forty years. Sidney was a thirty-second-degree Mason and moved to Peterborough, New Hampshire, in 1969, after having

Roger Wheeler with his proud mother, Florence, in Tulsa in 1976. (Courtesy Wheeler Family)

worked in Boston for forty years. Wheeler's mother's family had a New England history long enough for her to claim membership in the Daughters of the American Revolution as well as the Mayflower Society.[3] His mother, Florence, had attended Burdett College in Lynn, Massachusetts. She was a Congregationalist. With Sidney, the Wheelers had one daughter, Francis, and three sons, Roger, Alfred, and E. Sidney.

In that sense, Reading was an appropriate place for Wheeler to grow up. Settlers who were part of the Massachusetts Bay Colony petitioned in 1639 to establish a small town, called an inland plantation, named for Reading, England. When the American Revolution began, Reading provided a company of Minute Men to chase British soldiers after the opening skirmish of the war at Concord Bridge. By 1845, when the Boston and Maine Railroad came through, Reading had become a manufacturing center. Six years before Wheeler was born, Reading was a commuter suburb of seventy-four hundred people.

Published accounts say that Roger started his own neighborhood newspaper and a stamp-collecting service at fourteen. Two years later, he began hauling wood from Vermont back to Massachusetts using a truck that he bought on credit. In his Reading High School days, Wheeler was called Rog. According to the school's 1943 yearbook, bookkeeping was his favorite subject. That must have come in handy at the Reading Wood Company, which, according to his senior yearbook, Wheeler both managed and owned. His athletic strength was in cross-country. The class prophecy predicted he would be appointed forest ranger of Massachusetts.

Later, while serving in the Naval Reserve, he attended Notre Dame University. He graduated from Rice University in Houston, Texas, in 1946 with a BS in engineering.[4] There are several published versions of his early career. According to *New York Times* accounts, Wheeler worked for Gulf Oil in 1946, joined Standard Oil the next year, and moved to Tulsa, Oklahoma, by 1948. There, he was employed by the Cathodic Protection Company, which manufactured magnesium anodes, devices used to protect petroleum pipelines from corrosion.[5]

Wheeler saw an opportunity to earn more money by making his own anodes rather than buying them from outside sources. Since Tulsa was the Oil Capitol of the World, he moved there in 1948 with his wife, Patricia, found a mothballed smelting plant, and began melting surplus military equipment, such as airplane wheels, containing magnesium to pour anodes.[6]

In 1948, Wheeler earned about $32,000, as estimated in 2013 dollars. He quit Cathodic Protection and remained in Tulsa but lined up his own orders for the same product. In 1949, he founded the Standard Magnesium and Chemical Corporation, which he sold fifteen years later for $10 million, a value of $71 million in 2013.[7] Wheeler began working for Kaiser at Oakland, California, and briefly moved his family to Marin County, across the Golden Gate Bridge from San Francisco.

Soon, Wheeler put together a group of investors to bid on Telex, a Minnesota-based company, which made hearing aids and communications equipment such as speakers, headphones and microphones. In the dawn of the computer era, he saw an opportunity reminiscent of his anode-manufacturing brainstorm two decades earlier. As one acquaintance observed, "He was a driven and demanding man. That allowed him to do a tremendous amount."[8]

Telex Beginnings

Allen Hempel and Ralph Allison started Telex in 1936. The company was chartered in Minnesota as Telex, Incorporated, in 1940. Telex invented a portable hearing aid, consisting of an earphone connected to a protective case the size of a shoe box in which the user carried the contraption's necessary, rudimentary components. Telex branched into audio electronics and, by 1946, began marketing headsets.[9]

Wheeler became Telex chairman, chief executive, and the largest single shareholder in 1965. He took Telex into high-fidelity manufacturing and plug-compatible peripherals such as printers and tape drives, the predecessors of disk drives. Wheeler later claimed that the peripherals business had been developed at the suggestion of DuPont Corporation officials who had been unhappy with IBM equipment quality and prices.[10]

Although Telex manufactured a wide line of audio and electronic goods, by 1973, under Wheeler's leadership, computer products accounted for 69 percent of its revenues. At that time, IBM made about 74 percent of the tape drives used in industry, but Telex accounted for one-third of sales by independent tape-drive producers (IBM competition).

Wheeler's first major hire after the Telex purchase was Stephen Jatras, a Carnegie Mellon graduate who later earned a graduate degree at Massachusetts Institute of Technology. Earlier, Jatras had worked at Lockheed Electronics, where he headed the military systems division as vice president and general manager. He became Telex president in 1966.

Less than three years after Wheeler brought hot-shot engineering executive Stephen Jatras into the company as president, Telex became a serious contender in tape drives. When a recession began in December 1969, cost-conscious buyers began to look for inexpensive peripheral products, and Telex sales soared.

International Business Machines (IBM) dominated the computer market during the latter half of the twentieth century, including tape drives and other peripheral equipment. Often the size of a refrigerator—if not a phone booth—vintage tape drives were often arranged in linear banks, with some providing input to the computers, while others stored output. Drives performing these two functions were segregated into rows, called "banks," to enhance data processing speed. Tape drives were often the most expensive part of a computer system.

Wheeler hired away several IBM engineers to develop an interface that allowed Telex tape drives to connect to IBM computers at about half the price of the competing IBM equipment.

Flush with wealth, in the late 1960s Wheeler built a large house near one of the biggest mansions in Tulsa and also bought an 11,000-acre ranch in Wyoming to raise horses. Of course, he bought his own plane to shuttle between Tulsa, Wyoming, and Nantucket Island. One story related that big-time gamblers told him to have his horses lose sometimes, but he wouldn't do it. Wheeler supposedly refused to back off and play ball. He told one friend that gamblers said they were "gonna get him." According to this story, Wheeler said, "to hell with them." He wasn't going to worry about it.

A Dark Horse in a Tough Race

Forbes remarked in mid-March 1970 that in the previous year, Telex Corporation had shot up nearly 300 percent on the now defunct American Stock Exchange. Since moving to the New York Stock Exchange in January 1970, Telex had been on the list of most active NYSE stocks every week.[11]

Part of the reason for this success was micro targeting. Instead of maintaining a fancy publicity department in Tulsa, intensely private Roger Wheeler and Steve Jatras communicated directly with significant movers and shakers in the financial community, such as L. F. Rothschild and Company.

Initially, Telex manufactured privately labeled tape drives marketed by other manufacturers. But soon after Wheeler brought in Steve Jatras, Jatras's old employer, Lockheed, bought several tape drives, which were used to replace significantly more expensive, worn-out IBM equipment. Even before that, DuPont Corporation took several Telex tape drives on demonstration and then bought more.[12] DuPont officials were tired of paying too much for equipment that they considered overpriced.[13]

Unlike other IBM competitors such as Control Data Corporation, Telex established sales and service centers in some twenty major cities. They also claimed an improvement over the competing IBM product—Telex engineers developed a device that decreased friction and increased service life. And the price was right. Telex drives cost 20 to 50 percent less than comparable IBM replacements.

There was more. Telex used creative financing to sell the peripheral products and creative accounting methods, which *Forbes* described as "legitimate but not conservative," in order to book extraordinary profits.[14]

Wheeler and Jatras used equipment leasing to advantage Telex shareholders. In April 1969, Telex announced that virtually all tape drives currently leased to customers were being purchased by financial giant Transamerica. This gave the upstart Telex Corporation $5 million in extra cash—nearly $26 million in 2013 dollars. Better yet, after Transamerica's investment in each tape drive was recovered, Transamerica planned to share revenue with Telex.

Within weeks, Telex inked a companion deal in which Ezra Zilkha and other top-drawer New York investors, organized as Hudson Leasing, would pay Telex $10 million for new equipment leased to customers. Of course, it had to be built first. Telex had lined up $45 million in financing from Transamerica and $50 million from another financier to develop a second-generation disk drive that would process almost twice as fast as the contemporary state-of-the-art equipment.

Forbes assessed Telex two days before St. Patrick's Day in 1970. "It would be easy to dismiss Telex as just another highly leveraged stock heated up by fancy accounting," Forbes opined, yet it was "doing some highly interesting things—both technological and financial. It's a dark horse in a tough race, running against first-class competitors. But [Telex is] a much-better-than-average dark horse."[15] *Forbes* noted that Roger Wheeler was personally worth $60 million.

Tulsa insurance and convenience-store executive Burt Holmes encountered Roger Wheeler regularly during those years, when both men exercised almost every morning. Wheeler often ran at Southern Hills or in Tulsa's River Parks trails. Holmes noted that Wheeler was a gifted athlete, even in his mid-fifties.

Wheeler kept his hand in engineering years after he became an executive; he periodically provided technical directions to his staff at Telex.[16] Although he was usually demanding, there were exceptions. One new employee in the Telex shipping department recalled years later that she kicked him out of that department because he didn't have the required badge. Wheeler called her boss three times to make sure she wasn't fired. "She was just doing her job," Wheeler laughed. Steve Jatras described him as "smart, aggressive, and competitive," with high standards of personal ethics and morality." However, others described him as "a tough, contentious person to do business with, who sometimes created antagonisms" and that on occasion, he could be discourteous, abrupt, and obnoxious. By the early 1980s, he generally left day-to-day Telex operations to management.

All Business—Red-Headed and Born Again

When David Dixon left IBM for Telex in December 1971, he had no idea how challenging his next few years in Tulsa would be. "The Hill," as the Telex headquarters was known to those who put in fifty hours per week there, there was a boxy, nondescript high-rise building on a corner lot on the edge of town. Up on the top floor, in an office that was virtually all windows, Roger Wheeler had a good view of a sparsely developed commercial intersection.

Dixon's own digs were nothing to brag about, but Telex had lured him there from IBM with a 50 percent increase in his salary and an important promise: he could attend daytime engineering classes at the University of Tulsa as long as he put in forty hours per week as a service technician. His back story was not entirely unusual at Telex. David had worked for IBM for five years, mostly maintaining hardware and operating systems. Regarding his former company, he declared, "IBM only wanted a fair share of the business — all of it."

Now, his job was to help Telex compete with the Big Blue — as IBM was sometimes called because of its logo — by troubleshooting problems that caused Telex computers to break down. More than one Telex veteran recalled that IBM had superior products, but Telex effectively competed by providing superior service. Dixon helped that happen. Even though he was given daytime hours to complete his engineering degree as promised, his schedule, particularly on weekends, was harrowing. He logged seventy-five thousand miles of travel during his first year at Telex.

Wheeler was a very engaged manager when David arrived at Telex in 1971. Sometimes, it was rumored, Wheeler would stand on the Telex rooftop adjoining his office to take the names of late arrivals. Wheeler's meetings always lasted a half-hour or less, because people would come prepared. There were lots of office romances and divorces. Wheeler once threatened to get rid of all divorced employees because of the large number of office dramas. He even had an onsite pool cemented in after an after-hours party got out of hand.

David got his engineering degree but began to think about leaving Telex during the litigation with IBM. "The finance guy was calling around the country trying to scrounge payroll money," Dixon recalled. There were similar problems from time to time during the cash crunch in the mid-1970s. Several Telex engineers sent to work on a long-term project in Japan insisted on round-trip tickets before leaving; those who didn't do so had to return home at their own expense. David left Telex in November 1977.

Alan Holt, a Tulsa business owner, started working at Telex the year after David Dixon arrived. He remembered Wheeler as a demanding "all-business" executive. His office featured the usual executive amenities: a shower, fold-down bed, kitchen, and an ornately carved but well-used desk. Wheeler sported lots of expensive antiques, statues, and art. His subordinate executives worked one floor beneath Wheeler on "Mahogany Row."

Telex simply out-hustled IBM, placing a sales force in every major American metropolis and cutting prices. Alan Holt exemplified the can-do spirit of the Telex sales force, eventually grabbing the American Airlines account away from a complacent IBM sales executive.

By the time Jack Istnick arrived from Rochester, New York, to become the Telex director of marketing in 1977,

Christmas, 1977. Roger Wheeler jokes with his daughter-in-law.
(Courtesy Wheeler Family)

Roger Wheeler was more focused on his outside businesses than on Telex. They played golf from time to time, including a three-day tournament with Wheeler on Nantucket Island. The Roger Wheeler whom Istnick knew was soft spoken, matter of fact, and brief in conversation. There were the rumors that he could be a real jerk, but Istnick never saw it. Wheeler's was the first car in the parking lot every morning.

The Beginning of Negotiations

Roger Wheeler considered the signing of a contract to be merely the beginning of negotiations, at least according to several individuals who had heard as much from other businessmen who made deals with him. In the late 1970s, Wheeler made a deal to buy a new private plane, but found several errors in the written contract. Wheeler volunteered to have his secretary retype the documents to correct the errors. When the seller returned to pick up the contract, the errors had been removed, but Wheeler also had reduced the rate of interest on the balance due without bringing that revision to the seller's attention, or so the story goes.

Competing with IBM

Wheeler certainly may have liked Thomas J. Watson Sr., the founder of IBM. Watson and Wheeler definitely had some traits in common, if press reports are to be believed. "Watson had a fierce temper . . . an evangelist's fervor for business, and an unswerving compulsion to work."[17] While working for the National Cash Register Company, Watson had been convicted of an anti-trust violation in 1913 and sentenced to a year in prison, which he never served. He began running IBM instead. Under his guidance, clean-cut, white-shirted salesmen and engineers devoted to the

IBM "up or out" culture turned IBM into a leading world business, decades before the computer world emerged.

Watson's road to business success had not been entirely smooth, although, as one federal court noted in 1935, 36 percent of all tabulating machines, as well as a similar proportion of sorting machines and 82 percent of all punch-card devices were IBM products. The Roosevelt Administration charged both IBM and Remington Rand with anti-trust violations in the 1930s. One Justice Department anti-trust action was terminated by a consent decree twenty-one years after the government had attempted to curtail IBM's path to monopoly with little effect. IBM jealously guarded its competitive position in the computer industry, monopoly or not.

Control Data: The First Serious IBM Competitor

An entrepreneur named William C. Norris gathered a band of Wall Street-funded scientists who exploited advances in miniaturization of components and circuits well enough to show a profit by 1965. Control Data was the first IBM competitor to do so. Norris touted his proposed model 6600, which was to become "the largest computer in the world" until IBM announced it would produce its own model 6600, driving Control Data stock down from a lofty $161 per share to $32. Control Data complained, the government did nothing, and Norris filed suit in December 1968.

Due to new court rules allowing "discovery" of an opponent's factual evidence before trial, IBM yielded millions of pages of information. Control Data indexed these materials at an expense of $3 million. IBM settled the Control Data case in early December 1973, just before trial, giving up $110 million and a subsidiary, thus getting back the data which Control Data, Telex, and other litigants had been studying. This deal was struck just in time for Big Blue.

Fortune magazine reported that IBM erased, acid-bathed, and mulched every scrap of index, microfilm, paper, and tapes recovered from Control Data, rendering these materials useless for another lawsuit the government had filed in 1969. Judge David N. Edelstein, who was presiding in a 1969 federal government case against IBM, imposed a $150,000-per-day fine on IBM for failing to produce the requested documents, which the company defended during that Watergate summer by pleading attorney-client privilege and then getting another court to stay the fine.

Meanwhile, IBM teams analyzing data at their Armonk, New York, headquarters found alarming trends in the marketplace. The small-potato contenders for sales of "plug compatible" peripheral equipment were selling cheaper, more dependable products with revenues aggregating into about 10 percent of IBM's own $1.1 billion annual sales. And the competition was growing.

The Price War

IBM saw these competing peripheral suppliers, such as Roger Wheeler's Telex Corporation, as "parasites" manufacturing attachments that would not have any market at all without IBM's computers. Some IBM executives saw this competitive growth as a key corporate strategic issue that had to be dealt with—quickly. Thomas J. Watson Jr., son of the founder, developed the grand strategy. He told his IBM blue ribbon task force in 1971 that upstarts such as Telex were to be eliminated no matter what it cost.

IBM used a tactic copied from the 1950's gasoline price wars to do just that. Large oil companies charged deeply discounted prices until competing gas stations were wiped out. Thanks to this tactic, internal IBM analysts reported at the end of 1971 that Roger Wheeler's Telex and

Telex's principal competitor, Memorex, had fallen off the chart, losing as much as 62 percent of revenues. All this was accomplished in one operating year, taking Memorex from a $3.2 million net profit in 1970 to a $13.4 million loss in 1971. The IBM price cuts were designed, however reluctantly, by Berton Hochfeld, who counseled against such practices. By May 1974, competitors had lodged some twelve lawsuits seeking an aggregated $4.3 billion against Big Blue in various courts.

Maybe IBM executives didn't take Telex seriously. Through the years, however, Wheeler had developed "a penchant for instituting lawsuits which some associates described as 'disruptive.'"[18] He never tired of making money but rather, in his own words, got tired of being kicked around by IBM.

And so, in early 1972, the Big Blue had a major problem on its hands.

Chapter 5
Wheeler's Bluff

IBM is perhaps the best thing that has happened to America's legal profession since the invention of the courthouse.[1]

A year and a half later, Telex received a massive award that came just in time, or so it seemed. When federal judge A. Sherman Christiansen announced his decision in Tulsa on September 17, 1973, Telex had just spent $13.4 million developing a new mainframe to compete with IBM. At about the same time, customers began leasing peripheral equipment rather than buying it, portending potential financial disaster for Telex.[2]

Jackpot

That Monday, Judge Christiansen had awarded Telex $353 million, three times the actual amount of the harm Christiansen calculated IBM had caused Telex. It was the first time anyone had defeated the Big Blue in court on an anti-trust claim. One analyst told *Forbes* in September 1973, "It is the most significant antitrust decision to come along in years. This decision almost guarantees the long-term viability of other mainframe [computer] manufacturers."[3] *Fortune Magazine* remarked that, "Like Gulliver among the Lilliputians, International Business Machines is beset by a swarm of vengeful competitors who are trying to tie it down or break it up by antitrust decree. The recent judgment ordering I.B.M. [sic] to pay millions in damages to Telex, a money-losing manufacturer of peripheral equipment . . . has brought gleams to the eyes of numerous other companies who think they may also be able to collect."[4]

The Christiansen award was three times larger than Telex's assets and five times larger than their annual sales. The legal battle with IBM had consumed one year and seven months. It began with a lawsuit filed February 2, 1972, asking for "the dissolution of IBM as a single entity." Telex claimed that entity was monopolizing the electronic data processing (EDP) industry, asking for $877 million in damages, about $4.3 billion in 2013 money.

How It All Happened

The contest began with a federal judge in St. Paul issuing a temporary restraining order barring IBM from introducing a new product that allegedly would have crushed smaller competitors. The same judge resolved a number of preliminary issues in October 1972, setting the stage for a trial to begin in Tulsa on April 16 of the following year. The temporary restraining order was dissolved by an appellate court. IBM quietly filed a small counterclaim just before trial, alleging that Telex had breached a 1966 patent agreement.[5] Then, the litigation action moved to Oklahoma.

Anti-trust trials against big corporations were not unknown in Tulsa. Fifteen years before the Telex trial victory in Tulsa, "a cabal of east-coast lawyers" (along with some Tulsa attorneys) defending every major oil company in America filled every nook and cranny of federal judge Royce Savage's courtroom during a lengthy, non-jury trial. Savage dismissed the criminal charges at the end of the government's case.

When the trial against IBM began, Harry Ashbridge,

the first Telex witness, set the tone that led to victory. He lived forty miles south of Tulsa on a company ranch and hadn't seen much of it since the lawsuit was filed. Harry's confidence grew as he was examined by Telex attorney Floyd Walker was and cross-examined by IBM lawyers. However, once Harry finished his testimony, he walked off the stand and inexplicably left Telex to work elsewhere.[6]

About three months later, normally quiet and unassuming Telex president Steve Jatras predicted to reporters that "We're going to win big. Just wait and see." When the dispute began, Jatras took "total command of his company's IBM suit."[7]

Two years later, Telex attorney Floyd Walker told one reporter that he had wanted one thing when he started the Telex trial: enough money so that he could "piss on the oil men" of Tulsa.[8] And it almost happened.

Though Judge Christiansen ordered IBM to pay a substantial amount, the initial 1973 verdict had come at a cost. Jatras had devoted virtually all of his professional time the year before the trial to the case, while Telex's financial picture was worsening. Christiansen also found that Telex had misappropriated IBM trade secrets and owed IBM $21.9 million, about three million more than IBM had requested. This didn't surprise everyone. According to Telex urban legends, Jatras would bag IBM engineers, take them to Wheeler's Forty-First Street mansion and show them the cash.[9]

When the trial began, Thomas D. Barr, the IBM lead counsel, "... with his bulldog looks ... adopted the look, feel and inflection of the successful Eastern corporate lawyer." Few might recognize that this prototypical forty-two-year-old Yale law school prep hailed from Kansas City, Missouri. The red suspenders beneath his impeccable banker's blue suit were his only "down-home" touch.[10]

The Telex courtroom opposition consisted of general counsel Jack Bailey, attorney-engineer Serge Novovich and

Floyd Walker, who Wheeler once characterized as a "local yokel." After the trial, one newspaper reporter described Walker. "He is a good looking man, tall with chiseled features, whose friends claim resembled Doug Sanders, the professional golfer who won the U.S. Open at Southern Hills in 1958." When asked how he got started representing Wheeler, Walker candidly admitted, "I've never known why Wheeler picked me."[11]

Although he graduated second in his class, Walker lacked the social connections necessary to join a name firm in Tulsa. He worked as an insurance adjuster for a few years and then opened his own small law office, at first handling small personal injury cases but slowly, gradually, building a customer base and taking in more significant cases. He won a $600,000 judgment for a quadriplegic disabled in a truck accident and successfully prosecuted an oil fund swindle case that ultimately led to the removal of three corrupt state Supreme Court justices. Then, he occasionally began representing Roger Wheeler.

After Judge Christiansen granted Telex one of the largest judgments in American history to that date, IBM lawyers began the gritty motion-and-appeal work in the hushed law libraries. They considered Floyd Walker's award vulnerable.

A Little Confused

Time magazine sniffed on October 29, 1973, that the week prior, Judge Christiansen had seemed "more than a little confused," explaining that he might soon re-decide the amount of damages IBM would have to pay in the Telex case. *Time* noted that contrary to typical practice in such complex cases, Christiansen did not issue an initial opinion addressing whether IBM violated the law before proceeding further. Instead, he issued a single decision on liability and damages, which would have to be corrected. Floyd Walker, the Telex attorney, was hardly timid about the stakes.

Walker speculated that if forced to come up with $22 million for IBM, "there is no way Telex can stay out of bankruptcy and become any kind of viable competition."

Before IBM appealed to the Tenth Circuit Court of Appeals in Denver, Christiansen ruled that he had awarded Telex $100 million too much. Once the paperwork was compiled and filed, oral arguments in Denver were scheduled. IBM general counsel and former United States attorney general Nicholas D. "Nick" Katzenbach's presentation struck one observer as more like "a graduate [school] seminar." Several of the Supreme Court justices to whom Katzenbach argued had been vetted and approved by the Justice Department while he was the attorney general. Katzenbach's argument, although "not a flashy presentation was effective."[12]

The Tenth Circuit Court of Appeals in Denver heard oral arguments in May 1974. While waiting for the verdict, Rex Malik, a journalist who was writing a book on IBM, interviewed Wheeler. Malik observed that "On Roger Wheeler's desk stands a plaque carrying Santayana's aphorism, 'Those who do not remember the past are condemned to repeat it.' Roger Wheeler has no intention of doing so."[13]

In January 1975, the Tenth Circuit scrapped the multi-million-dollar bonanza and refused to rehear the case. Worse, they left in place the $21.9 million trade secret violation decision against Telex. The appellate court found that Christiansen mischaracterized the "market" for predatory practice analysis purposes. As a consequence, Christiansen had focused on too small a market. According to the Tenth Circuit, Christiansen had mischaracterized IBM's merely competitive practices as unlawfully predatory.[14]

Wheeler directed the Telex lawyers to file a writ of *certiorari*, asking the Supreme Court of the United States to review the case. Had Walker won, the $52 million-plus attorney fee to which he would have been entitled would have been the biggest fee ever paid to a single lawyer at that time. But even in mid-February 1975, *Forbes* reported, "Experts doubt that the Supreme Court will decide to hear Walker's appeal."[15]

On October 3, 1975, just three days before the Supreme Court would announce whether the Telex case against IBM was to be reviewed, the case settled without any money changing hands. An anti-IBM association spokesman called the settlement a "gross miscarriage" of justice that highlighted the need for legislation strengthening antitrust litigation. Other observers attributed the settlement to the precarious Telex financial condition. Since the company had become profitable in the prior year, the Telex executives decided not to "risk the company's future."[16] An IBM spokesman told reporters there was no point pursuing its espionage claim against Telex.

Computerworld told its industry readership that "People are the story here, not abstract legal principles," recalling that IBM's publicity initiative had "negated any possible public sympathy with startling—and often true—accounts about Telex's theft of trade secrets and espionage."[17] The magazine opined that the case "Encompassed the possibilities of good and evil on both sides; the issues of IBM's alleged marketing practices and Telex's alleged thefts showing the Janus-like nature of the industry in which right and wrong may be intertwined and possibly intermixed in the same organization."[18]

The $353 million was gone, but Telex was alive.

Roger Wheeler Tells All: The IBM Telex Backstory

After Telex had filed the lawsuit against IBM in 1972, Wheeler had turned down a confidential settlement offer that may have been as much as $10 million, amounting to more than $42 million in 2013 dollars.

Big Blue had gotten off scot free in the Telex litigation but was still looking at some $4 billion in lawsuits in late 1976 — real money back then.

Joseph C. Goulden, then an investigative reporter with three books under his belt, heard from Roger Wheeler in the summer of 1976 after the lawsuits were over. "Roger Wheeler, our board chairman, is excited that someone get into this story," a Telex representative told Goulden. "In fact, he is willing to send his jet to Virginia to bring you down here to Tulsa if you'll listen to us." Goulden climbed on the private jet and made the trip.

His description of Wheeler that summer is telling: "I met Roger Wheeler in his office in a low-slung building on the outskirts of Tulsa. Wheeler is a compact man in his early fifties; two or three heavy briefcases stand alongside his desk, and he occasionally brushes his hands over his tight curls as if to sweep away the pressures of running a half-dozen high-dollar enterprises simultaneously."[19]

Goulden described Wheeler as a New Englander by birth, an engineer by training, and a financier by choice. Despite the $106 million in revenue that Telex earned, Wheeler described the company as a sideline. "For the time and energy I've invested," he said, "Telex is a net loss for me." Regarding his Telex fight, he explained, "There's no way to compete on a head-to-head basis with IBM. It would be great to be the best company to compete, successfully, but a lot of pioneers come out with arrows in their butts—an empty bowl and unmarked grave. That's the fate of people who get out front."

Wheeler knew something about monopolies. He told Goulden that

After Rice, I started out in the oil business, shifted over to magnesium, and by the 1960s was the principal shareholder of Standard Magnesium and Chemical Company here in Tulsa. Dow [Chemical], our principal competitor, held an acknowledged monopoly in the industry, and it was doing business under a consent decree that said, in effect, its officers could be held in contempt of court if there were any violations and sent to jail.

The Justice Department would call me every few years and ask if Dow was doing anything wrong. Dow ran the kind of monopoly that didn't bother me as a competitor. Dow held the umbrella up there and kept the price right. Dow gave us technical advice when we got into problems. They were a benevolent monopolist.

Wheeler sold the magnesium business, by then located down the hill and a few blocks away from the Telex Corporation. The buyer, Kaiser Aluminum, acquired Standard Magnesium for stock shares then worth more than $8 million and found a spot for Wheeler in its San Francisco office. However, according to Wheeler, "I got bored. The atmosphere at Kaiser was competitive, but in a game I didn't wish to play. With all my stock, what did I have to gain?"

Meanwhile, M. E. Morrow, the chairman of a small electronics company called Telex Corporation, convinced himself that Telex "could be competitive with IBM," Wheeler recalled. The idea was to market peripheral devices, the gadgets through which problems and data were then fed into computers and stored after the data was processed. Printers were also considered to be peripheral equipment and represented about one third of IBM's total income by 1970.

The key for IBM's competitors such as Telex, Control Data Corporation, and others was to make sure that their equipment was "plug compatible," that is, designed so that the competitor's equipment could readily and easily be connected to IBM equipment.

When Du Pont asked IBM competitors for bids on equipment, Telex submitted a bid undercutting IBM's prices "substantially." Wheeler recalled later that he had invested in the company in 1965 at the prompting of Steve Jatras.

In a sense, Wheeler was in familiar territory when he

began competing with IBM, and said so years later in an interview. He claimed that in the mid-1960s, IBM's monopolistic umbrella served the same price-stabilizing function for the computer industry as Dow Chemical had for magnesium. "Oh boy, here's another opportunity to make a million. Here's another bird's nest on the ground," Wheeler recalled telling himself a decade later. IBM was so strong that it wouldn't worry about smaller companies "scrounging for scraps under the table." IBM would not cut prices to pick up the 5 percent of the market they didn't already own, or so Wheeler assumed. "Man was I wrong. I didn't know there was such a thing as a bad monopoly."

The United States government encouraged competition against IBM in 1970 when the Office of Management and Budget encouraged government agencies to look for peripheral suppliers other than IBM. But not even Wheeler predicted that there would be so many competitors for those "scraps under the table" available to small computer companies.

Wall Street investment bankers had little trouble seeing the coming situation. "There is a rule of thumb that a 10 percent penetration into IBM's competitive market causes IBM to react competitively . . . When IBM does decide to move in response to inroads to independents it is analogous to a card game in which IBM is the dealer and knows all the cards before they are dealt."[20]

By April 1971, Thomas J. Watson Jr., then serving as the IBM chief executive officer, emphasized that IBM must "swallow whatever financial pills [are] required for the future . . . irrespective of financial considerations for one or two years."

Five years later, Wheeler described how the IBM employees met this call. "When you boil it down, they actually made money by cutting prices . . . They altered service contracts and gave discounts for long-term leases, a lot of little gimmicks resulting in an effective price reduction of 50 percent. Then they raised their prices on the main frames [large computers only IBM provided] to offset the cuts." IBM was, according to Wheeler, ". . . ready to lose $400 million in one year with the knowledge that once we were smashed, they could gain $1.2 billion over the next three or four years."

This all surprised Wheeler, whose experience primarily had been based in Dow Chemical's "benevolent" monopoly. Wheeler fumed, "IBM was no such thing. I had bought a share of a riled-up bear. I couldn't believe what was happening." His Telex stock was worth at least $42 million—maybe more—when IBM struck. "When they gave us the first whack, we built a better mousetrap. The second time, it was tougher. The third time, it was so costly, so time consuming, that it was impossible. Your reaction time [for building competitive equipment] slows down from six months to two years."

Wheeler explained to Goulden, "I felt Telex could offer a better machine, and in fact we did, and at a better price. The problem was that it was very costly to develop the more sophisticated equipment, much more so than to improve upon the stuff that had been out on the market for eleven years." Many of the financial analysts echoed the comments of Goldman, Sachs, and Company, Inc., which stated that "IBM's long-term lease plan should siphon away so much Telex business as to preclude a positive investment attitude."[21]

The "Cinch Case" Begins

"Let's sue the bastards," Telex executives Steve Jatras and Richard Martin advised Wheeler. Earlier, Telex president Steve Jatras had called IBM general counsel Nick Katzenbach, whom he knew peripherally, and gently advised Katzenbach that IBM was violating antitrust laws.

Wheeler told an interviewer years later that "Katzenbach was a bit humble. He would see what could be done." Years later, Katzenbach told two courts that Telex was wrong.

In 1971, though, Katzenbach did nothing. Wheeler related, "he [Wheeler] did not want to resort to a lawsuit, even when his top management people said that IBM had stepped outside the law. We were in a highly competitive situation. We needed time and our total energies to get out of the trap. We couldn't do two things at once — run a lawsuit and run a business. Secondly, I didn't want the publicity. I was shocked at the headlines that eventually ran: Telex sues IBM."

Eventually, Wheeler decided to sue: "Another squeeze came from my lawyer [Floyd Walker]. He was writing letters for several months about how we should sue IBM and how we had a 'cinch case.'"

Walker had studied some research about IBM practices, which Steve Jatras had turned into a position paper; reviewed lawsuits that Control Data Corporation and other peripheral competitors had filed; and put together a twenty-nine page opinion letter. Walker believed that "IBM is vulnerable . . . for federal antitrust law violations" if Jatras's allegations against IBM were true. He proposed to keep the case as "small and simple as possible."

Wheeler didn't exactly jump on the opportunity to sue one of the largest corporations in the world. However, on December 7, 1971, Walker sent a second letter casually mentioning that Telex "probably has an obligation to itself and its stockholders" to sue. He was looking to collect as much as $36 million dollars (one third of which was actual damages) if he won the case. When Walker offered to do the lawsuit on a contingency with no significant Telex money advanced, Wheeler signed up.

"Go ahead, let's see what happens," said Wheeler. With that, Walker closed out the rest of his law practice, signed a contract with Wheeler on January 21, 1972, and filed the lawsuit against IBM.

Just as he had promised, Walker made every effort to keep the case small and simple, in order to keep out of the weeds where the IBM lawyers could ambush him. The strategy was to get to trial as quickly as possible. Unlike previous litigators, Walker limited the scope of the lawsuit, asking during discovery about "specific products and practices" within a given time frame. Walker described that approach later. "I interviewed former IBM employees who had planned or implemented specific projects, but in the end, three people gave me most of the input. Through them, I was able to identify . . . the documents I needed. Still, I ended up with 150 rolls of microfilm," Walker recalled in an interview.

"My approach was the rifle, not the shotgun. We would not play IBM's game and get bogged down in the paper chase. I've been the only lawyer suing IBM not to fall into that trap," he told Goulden five years later. "IBM would like to contest you on what I call 'the whole spectrum of the universe.' I aimed at three specific practices involving four or five products that Telex made. The rest of IBM's product line I ignored." Walker used these tactics for one overriding reason: "The game IBM plays is to overwhelm you. We wouldn't be trapped. We made few objections to their requests for discovery. It would take longer to object than it would to comply."

"If they wanted to take five depositions simultaneously, we let them . . . we just hired more lawyers." But there was another IBM discovery tactic that Walker had to accommodate. It was the war of attrition IBM waged, in Walker's opinion, when Walker began deposing IBM witnesses. "Depositions that should have taken two or three days dragged a week or more, with IBM witnesses seemingly unable to remember anything beyond their names and titles." Walker considered that he was coping with "the worst memories, or else the worst liars in Western civilization."

Ander Torgerson, who had studied IBM's competitors for Big Blue, claimed that he did not understand a question asking him whether he had heard or used the term "PCM," a standard industry acronym for "plug-compatible manufacturers" such as Telex. When Walker asked Torgerson about a complicated IBM marketing tactic dubbed "Mallard," Torgerson admitted being familiar with the term. "It's a kind of duck," the witness stated, relieved to at last answer one of Walker's questions.

The war of attrition was particularly useful to IBM for one reason: Telex was so low on cash that executives joked about "collecting from IBM posthumously."[22] That's when the list of witnesses willing to testify for Telex began to shrink. Floyd Walker claimed in one court brief that IBM had engaged in "an apparent concerted plan of tampering with [Telex] witnesses advising the court" and included "certain designated independent witnesses who were to testify based upon their extensive research and knowledge concerning financial information about IBM and Telex. After making the names of these witnesses known to IBM, there transpired a series of events so strange and coincidental, forming almost a pattern, as to cause Telex to inquire if there has not been a concerted effort on the part of IBM, it agents, and attorneys, and that these matters should be called to the attention of the court."

After giving the court one example concerning a suddenly unavailable witness named John Schmidt who worked in the data processing department of the long-defunct Midwest Stock Exchange Service Corp., Walker summarized what he was facing: "Suddenly, after filing the Telex final witness list, and without warning, they have declined to testify. The importance of these witnesses cannot be overestimated. Of the ten (10) witnesses (outside of Telex employees and agents) designated to testify in person, four (4) have suddenly indicated an unwillingness to testify. Of the seven (7) designated to testify by deposition, three (3) have now declined. It is inconceivable that IBM had nothing to do with this new development."

Checkmate

When, practically at the last minute, IBM hit Telex with a counterclaim, alleging that Telex had stolen IBM trade secrets, Floyd Walker wasn't all that surprised: "The counterclaim is a typical defense tactic in antitrust, for it gives the court a choice. Many a judge is known as 'half-a-loaf' which means he'll do something for both sides. I saw the counterclaim as an attempt to divert me from the main case, so I kept away from it as much as I could, and turned the defense [of the trade-secret counterclaim] over to another lawyer."

Judge Christiansen would have readily granted Telex more time to prepare for trial, but there was a problem. "We [the Telex lawyers] wanted it," Walker later recalled, "but Telex management, and I mean Wheeler, said a six-month delay would bankrupt Telex; they were on the ropes. I asked Telex outright whether it [the counterclaim] could be substantiated, and I was told no."

So Walker went to trial.

A Change of Strategy

The Big Blue's army was out-sized but flexible. Walker had to admire his opponents: "When IBM saw that their delaying strategy would not work, they changed. They accelerated, trying to put the trial on faster than I could get ready." Telex general counsel Jack Bailey had seen this strategy before.

"IBM spent money like it came from a Monopoly game," he recalled. "At one point they wanted a deposition from someone in Corpus Christi, Texas. IBM not only flew down a lawyer but also a clerk to wait around until the [court] reporter transcribed the proceedings so they could fly the transcript right back to New York. The thing only took thirty minutes, and it was never used in trial. But it meant I had to squander a day."[23]

The IBM lawyers hadn't counted on Walker's durability. His daily regimen shifted to living in his office on the twenty-second floor of the Fourth National Bank building in Tulsa, with a view of the courthouse. He worked at his office constantly, napping for a few hours in the early morning before starting all over again. Walker had lived this schedule before: "Work was never a stranger to me, even when I was a kid. What the dickens [sic] — I kept that kind of schedule to get through law school."

When the day arrived, the Big Blue was prepared. IBM leased thirty-five suites at the Central Plaza Apartments with thirty-five brand new Avis rental cars in the parking lot, just a few blocks away from the courthouse and even closer to the colonial-style, free-standing offices of their local counsel, Rucker, Tabor, McBride and Hopkins. Some six months earlier, the Tabor firm had begun amassing the paperwork necessary to fight Roger Wheeler's war — the documents, microfilm rolls, and deposition transcripts. Later, when the trial began, rush copies of the transcript were delivered to the Rucker offices twice daily. The platoon of some fifty IBM lawyers, supported by paralegals, administrative assistants, and clerks, checked every exhibit and testimony transcript — twice.

Thomas D. Barr, the lead IBM trial counsel, had many years of anti-trust experience. However, commanding the team of three hundred kept him from having the time to do what Floyd Walker did. "It may be pleasing to the ego to command those troops, but command is [itself] a distraction. There is nothing like steeping yourself in a case and using the very limitation of the human intellect to concentrate your attention and energies," one Tulsa lawyer observed.[24]

Walker's approach to winning the trial was simple. Among other documents, "He produced minutes of meetings of IBM's top management team . . . and the exhortation by Thomas Watson Jr. that IBM 'should make the hard decisions today' about 'dealing with' competitors." One internal IBM memorandum predicted that once confronted with IBM's new long-term lease program, a competitor such as Telex would become a 'Dying Company!'"

Walker used testimony from his live courtroom witnesses in Tulsa to bring such documents to life. He typically left the courtroom to prepare for later rebuttal testimony against IBM as another Telex lawyer defended the IBM counterclaim, alleging Telex trade-secret violations.

The IBM witnesses regarding the trade-secrets counterclaim produced page after page of testimony alluding to unlawful Telex hiring practices. Richard Moore was one such witness. He was working on IBM's "monolithic memory project" as an engineer when Telex offered him a $250,000 bonus if he could develop a copy of IBM's latest memory product within a year. Roger Wheeler offered Moore $15,000 — twice — if Moore would take the job on the spot, but the deal fell through when Moore refused to provide "technical information which he considered confidential to IBM."

Moore wasn't alone. Another IBM engineer named Richard Wilmer claimed that he was offered two $100,000 bonuses if he could duplicate an IBM system and have fifty-one units installed within twenty-eight months. Telex president Stephen Jatras was unenthusiastic about simply designing something better, Wilmer claimed, so Wilmer turned down the job. There was also testimony identifying several secret IBM codes found in Telex documents.

Betting Against IBM

After the trial ended in late May 1973, the highest verdict predicted in the Telex office pool was offered by Serge Novovich, an engineer who had become a lawyer and worked on the IBM case, at a massive $300 million. His boss, Jack Bailey, ". . . thought Serge was drunk, and he doesn't even drink." The next highest verdict after Serge's guess was $80 million.

Judge Christiansen's $352.5 million award made the Telex team look like pikers. The judge concluded in his 222-page opinion that Telex had lost $117.5 million as a result of IBM's antics: $70 million in market share, another $39 million in rentals, and almost $9 million in profits on sales.

The *Businessweek* reporter assigned to the trial couldn't help but notice that IBM lead counsel Thomas D. Barr "paled and strode from the room without comment" after he scanned the massive document.[25]

There was plenty of conversation at Wheeler's estate on Forty-First Street in Tulsa that evening. Someone had the *Tulsa Tribune* headline "Telex Awarded $352 Million" copied in five-by-seven-foot format, the size of two picture windows, and put one on either side of Wheeler's palatial front door. While the whoops and hollers echoed through the trees in the backyard, Floyd Walker calculated that Judge Christensen's award to Telex was going to mean $50 to $60 million in his pocket.

Collecting

In all the celebrations during those first giddy days after the judge's decision, hardly anyone at Telex or in the business press really focused on Christiansen's $22.9 million award in IBM's favor. But Wheeler did, and with good reason. It was one thing to be awarded $352.5 million of IBM money, but another thing to collect it.

Wheeler's gamble hadn't yet paid off, and Telex was practically out of cash. The company had lost $13.3 million when the books closed on the fiscal year ending in March 1973. Since Telex owed millions in bank loans, Wheeler began talking to anti-trust experts. One of them was a California lawyer named Maxwell Blecher, who told Wheeler that "if he had a chance to settle the case he should grab it."[26]

Although Walker had been thinking along the same lines and had called Barr shortly after the $352.5 million award, urging him to settle now (if the case were to be settled at all), Walker was not prepared for what happened next.

Wheeler had called IBM president Frank M. Cary, asked him if he wanted to settle the lawsuit, and then made arrangements to meet without the lawyers. When they met at a nondescript motel near the St. Louis airport, Wheeler had been briefed by Walker, who, according to Wheeler, told him not to take a dime less than $350 million. But Walker later remembered telling Wheeler that the figure should be a starting point for negotiations.

Whatever Wheeler was told, he opened with a firm $350 million offer to settle the case, Cary countered with a vague hint of paying about $100 million. After a long silence, Wheeler and Cary agreed to meet again "sometime."

More than one sideline handicapper has insisted in the years since that Wheeler had made a serious tactical blunder by insisting on the full Monte, given that Blecher and others had told him no federal appellate court in America would affirm a $352.5 million award. Yet, four years later, Wheeler refused to second-guess himself. "Things were happening pretty fast," Wheeler remembered. "I had to go with Floyd Walker. Floyd felt, in the first place, that we could get a monetary recovery, when the rest of us were thinking mainly in terms of [injunctions]. Walker wanted to sue when a lot of people here [at Telex] were saying just the opposite. It was Walker's show. It seemed to make sense."

Perhaps it did make sense—at least until October 9, when Judge Christiansen declared, in response to an IBM motion for a new trial, that there was a problem with his calculations, as Thomas Barr chortled to the press. One month later, when Christiansen revised his award, Telex was still to the good by $259.5 million, less IBM's $22.9 million counterclaim, of course.

While Telex and IBM waited for the Tenth Circuit Court of Appeals in Denver to sort it all out, Wheeler began to have second thoughts about his victory. "I am a capitalist, and I have investments in the market myself," he observed. "The Wall Street analysts were yelling that our lawsuit was responsible for the crash [in computer stocks]. I said to myself, 'If the alternative is creating a major depression, I'd rather let Telex go down the tube," particularly since whatever else the outcome, the Telex victory "did bring about competition — which is what this country is all about."

The afternoon of Friday, January 24, 1975, Wheeler was in the Summit Club on the thirty-second floor of the Fourth National Bank building when he received a phone call. Floyd Walker, whose office was ten stories below the Summit in the same building, had learned that the Tenth Circuit would be announcing its decision that afternoon. Wheeler took the elevator downstairs and waited in Walker's office.

Jack Bailey was on his way back to Tulsa from New York. The Telex lawyer and a handful of other executives were returning from an unsuccessful effort to talk the New York Stock Exchange officials out of "delisting" the company because of its diminished revenues. During a refueling stopover, one of the men went into the terminal, called home to report his ETA in Tulsa, and received the bad news. The Tenth Circuit had thrown out the decision against IBM but kept the $22.9 million decision against Telex in place.

"Christ, I couldn't believe it," Wheeler ruminated the next summer. "I was sick. I came back to the [Telex] plant in a daze, listening to the news over and over again on the car radio. It was like hearing your own death knell." Telex executives and secretaries alike stood around crying, according to one observer.

In sum and substance, according to the Denver appeals court, Judge Christiansen had defined the market IBM was accused of monopolizing too narrowly; the relevant market for monopoly purposes, according the Denver judges, was not just the products compatible with IBM products, as Christiansen had ruled, but all peripheral products, compatible with IBM or not. Oddly, internal IBM views on this point, as revealed in discovered documents, were more consistent with the Telex argument than the Tenth Circuit decision.

Fortunes are made and lost on such legal distinctions.

Since the Tenth Circuit let the $22.9 million judgment against Telex stand, Telex was now $100 million in debt, almost one third of which was overdue. Telex could not even pay for an appeal bond, but Judge Christiansen waived the requirement so that Telex could ask the Supreme Court of the United States for a third opinion by a writ of *certiorari*. The Supreme Court wasn't obligated to hear the case, but Telex had no choice but to ask.

When Wheeler hired appellate court specialist Moses Lasky, "we rapidly approached the point where the lawyers would get all the money, if we won," a Telex executive later claimed. In San Francisco and elsewhere, Lasky was known for his skills writing appellate briefs. His typical arrangement was $25,000 up front ($105,000 in 2013 value) and another $15,000 if he later won the Supreme Court argument. Should he obtain a new trial or a reinstatement of the $259.5 million, Lasky would be paid 5 percent of the first $100 million recovered, up to $5 million. There was, after all, no need to be greedy.

Telex also asked the Justice Department to file an *amicus curiae* brief supporting Telex. The lower level government lawyers were enthusiastic, but nothing happened.

Meanwhile, as the briefing process droned on during the summer, Jack Bailey became increasingly concerned. "We were going up before 'the new Nixon court' and I thought about it a lot—especially late at night—and decided our chances were maybe 5 percent. Lots of things were happening. Justice Douglas should be a Telex vote, but he was in and out of the hospital. I felt the tilt was heavily against us."

The Telex loan officer at Continental Illinois Bank in Chicago had his neck on the line. He knew that if the Telex appeal to the Supreme Court was unsuccessful, in the words of Roger Wheeler, all the banks would receive in repayment would be "a bankrupt computer company — less of course the $20-odd million we'd be paying IBM."

Wheeler seemed to withdraw from his legal team, at least according to Walker, who later claimed that "Wheeler was not listening to the lawyers most intimately involved in the case — Moses Lasky and me. He would talk to lawyers literally on the street corner and ask what they thought the Supreme Court would do. He would call up prominent lawyers he didn't even know and ask the same question."

Then he made the telephone call.

"We'll take $15 million," Wheeler told IBM president Frank M. Cary, who probably stifled a snicker or two before saying, "Under no circumstances will we give Telex any money. Our thinking is that you should pay IBM $3 million." That ended the conversation.

Two days earlier, on September 10, Wheeler had asked IBM in writing to resume negotiations. Telex didn't have much choice, given that earlier that summer the Securities and Exchange Commission had forced Wheeler to circulate an auditor's advisory opinion stating that Telex would not survive if forced to pay the $22 million claim. So now, after the Cary turn-down, Wheeler and Bailey met with former federal judge and past general counsel of the Gulf Corporation, Royce H. Savage, as well as future federal judge James Ellison, a corporate reorganization and bankruptcy specialist. Savage and Ellison knew what to do.

By September 30, at Savage's prompting, IBM general counsel Nicholas Katzenbach was on his way to Tulsa. The previous day, the Supreme Court had begun the process of winnowing down the cases they would accept for consideration.

The settlement conference in Judge Savage's office the

morning of Wednesday, October 1, was attended by some eight lead attorneys and executives. Floyd Walker and Moses Lasky, the lawyers who had done the heavy lifting in court, were not among them. The morning session began on a discouraging note, so far as Telex was concerned. IBM wanted $15 million, although some of it could be paid on an installment plan, perhaps through promissory notes. Telex general counsel Jack Bailey rejected the pitch out of hand. "No employee of Telex had any interest in working for IBM, which we would be doing if we made a profit only to pay them." Bailey countered with a wash in which neither company would pay anything.[27]

The IBM lawyers retreated to local counsel's office several blocks away, but one of them returned around noon with some somber news. The case had been decided in some fashion the previous day by the Supreme Court in Washington. So if Telex and IBM were going to withdraw their cases against each other and settle, the Supreme Court had to be notified no later than noon the next day.

IBM agreed in principle that Thursday to Jack Bailey's proposed "wash settlement" with no money changing hands, but not until after the Thursday noon deadline had passed. In fact, Wheeler's last look at the paperwork happened at 1:00 a.m. Friday morning in his offices at Telex. But the proposed IBM press release, which referred to the "theft of valuable trade secrets," nearly killed the deal. Instead, IBM and Telex issued separate but mutually agreed-upon press releases.

The Triple Mystery—A Supreme Court Leak?

When Joseph Goulden interviewed Roger Wheeler in Tulsa, he quickly learned why the Telex jet had been sent to pluck him out of the Blue Ridge Mountains. Wheeler wondered whether Wall Street "in ways both subtle and direct prompted the [Tenth Circuit in Denver] to decide his case on grounds totally unrelated to anti-trust. . . . In this case, the circuit court followed the stock market tables," Wheeler claimed. But there was something else — something potentially explosive.

Wheeler believed that IBM had known in advance that the Telex's writ of *certiorari* had been granted by the Supreme Court. He was relying upon the analysis of Telex's Washington counsel, Gilbert Cuneo, who had overheard some casual conversation between a Supreme Court employee and an IBM attorney at the court building, which convinced Cuneo that this might be so. But, according to Wheeler, Cuneo advised him later that he met with Chief Justice Burger and Justice Brennan, then the most senior member of the court, who assured Cuneo that the Telex writ of *certiorari* had been denied.

Still, three questions had not been answered satisfactorily. Had there been a leak at the Supreme Court? Perhaps more importantly, had IBM discovered the Telex writ of *certiorari* was going to be denied? If so, why on earth would IBM let Telex off the hook after four years of expensive litigation and adverse publicity?

The last question is perhaps the most perplexing. Goulden quoted an unnamed source "on the periphery of the case" who thought he had the answer to why IBM might have settled out of court and let Telex off the hook. "IBM management is sophisticated enough to realize the public relations consequences of totally destroying Telex, which is what would have happened had Telex stuck with the suit and lost."

"The death of Telex would confirm what IBM critics have been saying, that it is a 'monster corporation capable of smashing anyone in its way.' It makes about as much sense for IBM to take $20 million or so off Telex as it does for Willie Sutton [who robbed banks because 'That's where the money is'] to steal a school kid's lunch money. IBM takes its win and goes on to other things. Telex 'survives' and the fact that it exists helps keep up the fiction that there is 'competition to IBM.'"

"We'll never know, will we?" Goulden's anonymous source continued. "Maybe Katzenbach [the IBM general counsel] will write his memoirs when he is an old man."

He didn't. Katzenbach died in May 2012.

What Legal Fees?

When Roger Wheeler asked Lasky to write and file a single brief in the Supreme Court of the United States, Telex agreed to pay Lasky if Telex was successful. When Telex settled with IBM, the company offered him 10 percent of what, in Lasky's view, Telex owed. Instead of accepting, Lasky took Telex to court and won.

It had all started earlier in 1975 when Roger Wheeler recruited Lasky to save Telex by writing the brief to get Telex in front of the Supreme Court. Lasky had spent some forty-five years in a leading San Francisco law firm developing a reputation that brought Wheeler to his door.

Lasky agreed to take the briefing assignment for a percentage of any settlement offer generated after the offer was filed, with a $5 million ceiling—on one little condition. Lasky was to get at least $1 million as part of any IBM settlement in addition to his $25,000 starting retainer.

Lasky was in the Telex boardroom in Tulsa that September 1975 when Wheeler decided to do a wash settlement with IBM. Each company would drop their cases. There was of course one catch. Lasky reminded Wheeler that "even if the two lawsuits were dropped, Telex would owe him $1 million for having filed his brief." The silence was overwhelming. "Is that right?" Wheeler asked his own company lawyer, just before throwing a pencil at him.

Goulden also discussed legal fees with Floyd Walker in Walker's office two years after his $50 to $60 million contingency fee had flown away. The October 1975 settlement discussions with IBM came up first. Walker had not even been involved, despite the four years he had devoted to the case. Walker's version of the argument with Wheeler is worth describing. According to Walker, Wheeler claimed that Walker urged him to continue the litigation only because Walker wanted his $50 million fee, while Wheeler had to consider the survival of Telex.

"Roger twisted the factual situation to suit whatever his purpose was at the moment. He urged [Walker to accept] the contingency [fee] contract to give me the greater incentive to do the best thing for Telex. Then he used the [contingency fee] contract's existence so he could say my financial interest meant my advice was no longer objective."[28]

Since Truman Rucker, the local IBM counsel, knew that Walker and Lasky were mad, he had insisted that in the final IBM-Telex document Wheeler would personally indemnify IBM against any claims Walker or Lasky might make later for legal fees.

Walker argued that his contingency-fee contract with Telex should be applied to the trade-secrets judgment that Telex had avoided paying, entitling Walker to about $1.4 million. He also claimed as a backup argument that, in any event, he deserved to be paid for the value of his services, some $2.5 million.

"A contingency agreement is a gamble," countered Telex general counsel Jack Bailey in a separate interview. "Walker could have signed on for a flat fee, but he chose the other route. Now he's trying to change the rules." Telex argued in court that since Telex didn't have money to pay the IBM counterclaim at the time, Walker deserved no fee. Beyond this, Wheeler, through Telex, charged that Walker had not paid enough attention to the IBM trade-secrets counterclaim. Since Walker was not the skilled antitrust attorney he had represented himself to be, Telex contended, he should pay Telex the $939,000 Telex spent in out-of-pocket expenses prosecuting the case.

This did not endear Walker to Wheeler, who Walker

claimed interfered in the case to the point he became a pest. Walker talked him into taking a month-long cruise during the trial. "Otherwise," Walker carped, "he'd have had his finger in everything."[29]

"Floyd the Giant Killer," as *Fortune* magazine had touted Walker in an October 1973 article, had a few months to dream about the $50 million. He told *Fortune* that he didn't plan to change his lifestyle, although he did buy a nice home on Keystone Lake, west of Tulsa. But now, in the summer of 1976, during the Goulden interview, Walker recalled that he had wanted to establish an endowment at the University of Tulsa Law School, create trust funds for his children, and practice law "a heck of a lot less and [devote] much of my time to managing money." But, Walker concluded, ". . . you don't get excited when one slips away from you."

How'd I Do?

Today, Joel Wohlegemuth is a super lawyer, a sixtyish-year-old name partner in one of Tulsa's most powerful and prestigious law firms with fancy offices on the twenty-ninth floor of the Mid-Continent Tower. From his suite of offices, one can easily see the low hills and plains that surround the mid-sized city once called the "Oil Capitol of the World." With good binoculars, you can see the place Wohlgemuth nearly died with Roger Wheeler thirty-two years ago.

Wohlegemuth graduated from the law school at Washington University in St. Louis and took a job with Douglas M. Head, the last Republican attorney general of Minnesota. He married "a local girl," moved to Tulsa in 1971, and heard from Roger Wheeler seven years later after winning a $2.5 million jury verdict in an anti-trust case that was eventually settled. Wheeler called Wohlegemuth late on a Friday afternoon with a proposition. The good news was that Wheeler wanted Wohlegemuth to file a case against a powerful Fortune 500 company and request an injunction. The bad news was that it had to be done the following Monday.

Wohlegemuth worked the entire weekend, filed the case, resolved the dispute to Wheeler's satisfaction, and soon became a frequent flyer on a Telex Corporation plane traveling with Wheeler and Telex general counsel Jack Bailey to Washington, DC, on a highly sensitive matter.

Wheeler was being investigated by the Securities and Exchange Commission (SEC) for improperly charging personal expenses to Telex Corporation. Stanley Sporkin, the SEC enforcement chief, "had it in for Wheeler," the Telex attorneys thought, and wanted a consent decree in which Wheeler admitted guilt. Joel and Wheeler flew up to Washington five or six times to deal with the charges.

There were a few arguments along the way. Wheeler was a sometimes difficult client with a legendary temper. He fired the Telex general counsel once and Stephen Jatras, his second-in-command, six times for insisting on going forward with the SEC settlement, but eventually relented. When Wheeler lost his temper, Wohlegemuth simply let him vent, then reasserted whatever point had set Wheeler off in the first place. Usually, Wheeler would simply say, "I understand," and let it go.

Jack Bailey, the Telex general counsel, wanted these SEC charges resolved. And so, some sixty to ninety days before Wheeler was murdered, Wheeler, Tulsa attorney Fred Dorwart, and Wohlegemuth traveled to Washington on Wheeler's jet and met with Stanley Sporkin, the SEC director of enforcement, who later served as CIA general counsel and a federal district court judge.

The SEC office was a massive chamber with chairs arranged in a semi-circle facing a couch, where Sporkin sat by himself. Once the meeting began, however, Wheeler got up from his assigned straight-backed chair and sat next to Sporkin on the couch.

"I've been harassed," Wheeler began, completely

disregarding the strategy he and his attorneys had agreed upon before the meeting. He harangued Sporkin for ten minutes before pausing. "That's all I have to say," He said, and walked out, leaving Bailey, Wohlegemuth, and Dorwart to face Sporkin. The attorneys found Wheeler afterwards walking around the block.

"How'd I do?" Wheeler smirked.

With that, the real work began. Dorwart and Wohlegemuth stayed behind to discuss a possible deal before leaving for the airport. Joel was paged at Dulles and asked to submit a proposal by May 28, 1981. The deal had gone through four revisions by May 27.

Wheeler called Joel that morning and asked him to play golf at Southern Hills. "Make a fourth with us!" Wheeler suggested, but Joel had to decline in order to finish drafting the proposed consent order that was due the next day.

At 5:15 p.m., he began the twenty-minute drive from downtown Tulsa to the Telex building with the draft settlement in his briefcase. While in the car, he heard on the radio that there had been a murder at Southern Hills. It didn't occur to Wohlegemuth that this might have been Roger Wheeler. But within a mile of Telex, it was clear that Roger Wheeler had been murdered. Joel went home and called Fred Dorwart with the news. Only later did Wohlegemuth realize that he himself might have been a second victim, since he would have met Wheeler at Telex for the ride to Southern Hills.

Only a few days before the murder, while working on the SEC settlement at Wheeler's office, Wohlegemuth overheard one side of a conversation about World Jai Alai that hinted at the problems Wheeler had uncovered in the gambling business he had acquired. "I just can't believe it!" Wheeler said, just before he abruptly dropped the subject.

Chapter 6
Whitey's Way

South Boston is set up like a slice of pie. And the projects, set at the bottom of the hill like the last piece nobody wanted sucked a--. Drug dealers, thugs, bangers, con-men, thieves, and addicts preyed on the hard-working people stacked up in the concrete buildings. The projects were full of everybody you either didn't want to know or didn't give a crap about in the first place.[1]

In 1979, Whitey Bulger ascended to leadership of the Winter Hill gang in unusual circumstances. Howie Winter and his entire management cadre, except for Bulger and Flemmi, had been rolled up and jailed for fixing horse races. The fact that Bulger and Flemmi were named as unindicted co-conspirators and left on the street was no coincidence.

By that year, a problem was brewing sixteen hundred miles away in Tulsa for Winter Hill wannabe John B. Callahan and Bulger himself. That problem was another hard-charging, all-business Boston native three years older Whitey's senior who ran the Telex Corporation—Roger Wheeler. As John Callahan put it, ". . . this guy won't take our money. We need to get rid of him. Can you help us?"[2] It wasn't that simple. The mob tried to avoid hits on "legitimate" citizens, not for moral reasons but because such killings invariably brought swarms of police. The law was little concerned with a gangland killing; they (generally) were difficult to solve and, as the ordinary copper would say, "Who cares?"

Still, Whitey and Stevie bought into this murder, presumably for the substantial amount of money that they might get their hands on, which outweighed the danger from the police. Besides, there was always FBI agent John Connolly in their pocket. What the mob couldn't cover up, he could.

Some believe that Whitey was already receiving part of the World Jai Alai skim before Wheeler was killed. According to this theory, an audit that Roger Wheeler had planned might have led to Callahan and, through him, to Stevie and Whitey. That would be wholly unacceptable, so Whitey planned the hit in a way so that he wouldn't get his hands dirty. Whitey arranged the actual work to be done by big John Martorano, a competent and experienced assassin.

At the same time, some contend that Whitey was reluctant to sanction the Wheeler hit, even with the motivation of another stream of revenue, but was eventually persuaded by H. Paul Rico and Callahan.

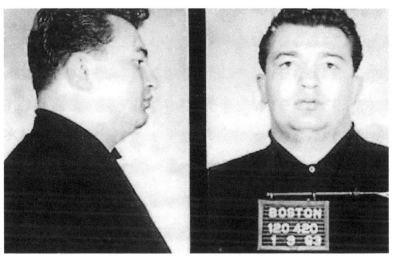

Hitman John Martorano. (Courtesy Boston Police)

Murder in the Course of Business

Whatever Bulger's motivation, the Wheeler murder was just another business tactic, another way that the mob in Boston, Irish and Italian alike, created opportunities for itself in the world of commerce. When the mob coveted something owned by somebody else, they took it. Cooperation was easiest, through cutting in the mob for a percentage of the operation. It was pure profit for the gangsters, since the business owner did all the work.

Three years later, in January 1984, Whitey decided to go into the liquor business with his protégé Kevin Weeks, but no "civilians" were to be involved. Whitey went to the modest walk-up apartment that Stephen "Stippo" Rakes and his wife, Julia, rented. He held their young daughter while sitting at their coffee table and talked a few minutes about what a shame it would be if her father didn't live long enough to see her grow up. Within a few days, Stippo's Liquor Store, in which Stephen and Julia had invested their life savings, had become the South Boston Liquor Store, owned by Whitey Bulger and Kevin Weeks. For a purchase price of $64,000, the Rakes lost money but escaped with their lives. Kevin Weeks claimed in his memoirs that the sale was voluntary, but the courts found otherwise.

That same year, FBI agent John Connolly claimed in a report to his Washington superiors that Bulger had given him information of superior value resulting in "an enhancement of the overall TECIP [Top Echelon Criminal Informant Program] and the general objectives of the FBI."[3]

That had long been the way of things in Boston, the home and playground of what the press referred to as the Irish mob. If the mob couldn't get what it wanted by forced cooperation, they resorted to beatings, mutilations, and threats. Murder was the ultimate commercial weapon.

Irish organized crime in Boston had never been the well-disciplined criminal monolith that the Italian Mafia was, nor was it entirely Irish. The Irish gangs were Irish in both spirit and composition but ethnically diverse. If you were Italian but ruthless enough, you might qualify for a spot in gang leadership. Steve Flemmi was of Italian blood, as was assassin John Martorano, although his mother was Irish. By 1981, Whitey had worked for some sixteen years in assorted Irish gangs in Boston.

Irish gangsters in Boston fought each other with regularity, but mostly they pushed other people around to protect their own interests. Anybody that got in the way was in trouble. Their gods were money, prestige, power, and bragging rights, any way they could get them. The dead left behind were mostly other gangsters, bookies, and fences whose death or disappearance didn't bother the general public or the authorities. The Wheeler murder was just another chapter in the foul history of the Irish gangs.

Taking Care of Business

Now, after the Wheeler murder, threats and violence were the cornerstones of Whitey Bulger's life. Not only was it an expedient way to generate and keep business, but Whitey found it personally satisfying. He liked to hurt people and watch them cringe in fear. He also enjoyed killing. The word quickly spread that he was a bad man to have as a competitor.

Crime, like any other enterprise, has to be carefully and persistently tended to achieve success. Even after Whitey had climbed to the top of the heap, there were constant demands on his time and energy. There were threats, real or imagined, not only to his supremacy but also to his freedom, and these had to be dealt with quickly and in whatever way was most expedient.

The most frequent way of dealing with threats was murder. Take the July 1982 assassination of John Callahan, a Southie boy and long-time confederate of Whitey's. Callahan had been very useful to Whitey in the Wheeler affair, providing him with inside information. He was a Yale-degreed CPA who liked to associate with South Boston gangsters. He had, as a Boston cop neatly put it, "a bad case of gangsteritis."[4] Callahan had even shared a condo in Florida with John Martorano and an apartment with John's brother, Jimmy the Bear.

Through his connections with the First National Bank of Boston, Callahan became associated with World Jai Alai (WJA). He became president in 1975 but had to step down when authorities discovered he was associating with organized crime figures. He, in turn, hired H. Paul Rico as vice president for security, having retired from the FBI that year. Rico immediately began wooing the local FBI, sponsoring all-expense-paid junkets to the Bahamas for several agents. Rico was the perfect choice: he had connections on both sides of the law and used those to the benefit of Callahan, Bulger, and the Winter Hill boys.

Then, when WJA branched out from its frontons in Miami and Tampa into Hartford, Connecticut, Wheeler suspected a skimming operation, probably through Callahan and maybe Rico. At the urging of Callahan, the Boston gang was looking at a healthy take — an estimated $10,000 per month — which would have become one of the most profitable scams Winter Hill ever had.

After the May 27, 1981, Wheeler killing, Callahan became a liability to Winter Hill. If he talked to investigators probing the WJA mess, there could have been big trouble leading right to Whitey's door. Once Brian Halloran was murdered as well, Callahan was the last loose end potentially tying Bulger and Flemmi to Wheeler's murder.

So, in the last dark hours of July 31, 1982, John Callahan met the same end to which Whitey and Flemmi had consigned so many others. Callahan had flown in to Fort Lauderdale with some money for John Martorano. Martorano met him in the airport, carried his luggage to a van, and then shot him in the back of the head as he settled into the front passenger seat. Joe McDonald watched from a second car nearby. When Martorano and McDonald were transferring Callahan to the trunk of his own Cadillac, Callahan began moaning, so McDonald shot him in the head again. The hit men left Callahan's wallet in the men's room of a bar in little Havana and dumped the car at the Miami airport.[5] The murder followed the same pattern that had worked so well in the past, including that of Roger Wheeler the previous year.

Even before the killing, Whitey had been busy misleading law enforcement, as was his common practice. FBI agent Connolly had floated the intentionally vague story that Callahan had some problem with "a Cuban group who impressed him as being very bad."[6] In the murder business, it was always best to nominate possible suspects who were not only likely but also far away, unconnected, and preferably vague. The line about "a Cuban group" that was "very bad" fit the model perfectly.

On August 3, 1982, a parking attendant at the Miami airport noticed blood running from the trunk of a silver Cadillac. Callahan, quite dead, had been locked inside, with two bullet holes in his head and a dime on his chest.

Tulsa Homicide detective Mike Huff had been on Callahan's trail the very month Callahan was killed. Earlier in July, Huff and his partner had flown into Hartford to meet with Connecticut state police investigators. The entire entourage drove to Boston in search of Callahan, who was nowhere to be found.

Since they were in Boston anyway, the investigators met with Jeremiah T. O'Sullivan, then serving as chief prosecutor for the New England Organized Crime Strike Force. O'Sullivan casually disclosed some information that Huff had been trying to uncover for over a year. O'Sullivan revealed that Halloran, who could potentially have unlocked the Roger Wheeler case, had been debriefed and unceremoniously dumped instead of being placed in the US Federal Witness Protection Program. O'Sullivan offered no apologies for failing to brief Connecticut or Oklahoma authorities on these developments. Later, Massachusetts state troopers discovered that Callahan and Halloran shared a cheap condominium near Plantation, Florida. Halloran also had access to the safe in Callahan's Boston office.

In September 1982, FBI Agent John Morris closed Flemmi's status as an informant, recording that Flemmi was a suspect in the New England Mafia investigation when, in fact, Flemmi had been acting as an informant in that matter. Later review of FBI records revealed that Flemmi met with FBI agents some forty-six times during the three-year period after his status as an informant was closed.

Meanwhile, Connolly did not bother to close Bulger's informant status. In April 1983, Connolly documented the real reason Flemmi had been dropped from the informant program, at least on the FBI books. Flemmi "was under active investigation" for the Roger Wheeler and John Callahan murders.[7] That very month, the Oklahoma City FBI agents charged with investigating the Roger Wheeler murder asked for permission to interview Bulger and Flemmi but were denied access. Seven months later, however, on November 3, 1983, Special Agents Montanari and Leo Brunnick were finally allowed to meet Bulger and Flemmi in connection with their investigation of the Roger Wheeler murder.

The interview in South Boston was highly unusual in two respects. First, contrary to standard law enforcement procedure, Bulger and Flemmi were interviewed together, allowing them to buttress their separate stories. Second, neither Bulger nor Flemmi were required to take a lie detector test, contrary to FBI standard procedure.

That made things easier for Bulger, who argued that neither the Wheeler nor the Callahan murder made any business sense for Winter Hill. He also said that he had no business relationship with Callahan or anyone else at WJA.

In effect, Bulger argued that such a relationship would have been mob malpractice in that "it is not the style of either Bulger or Flemmi to be involved in any criminal activities that they cannot control completely." Furthermore, "they generally feel that they could not exercise sufficient control over things outside their own geographical area," which would have contradicted any involvement in WJA.[8]

Moreover, Bulger continued, "it would be nonsense to think that he and Flemmi were getting any skim out of WJA because they have nothing to show for it." To support his claim, Bulger complained that a $250,000 debt to the Patriarca family he and Flemmi had "inherited" from Howie Winter when Howie went to prison remained mostly unpaid.

Still, Gerry Montanari pressed on. One day in the spring of 1983, when he opened his World Jai Alai murder files in the Boston FBI office, he found the unexpect Renee Frilot Graf ed. Someone had rifled through the papers and misfiled some documents, while others were missing altogether.

When Montanari complained to Bob Fitzgerald, the Boston special agent in charge, Fitzgerald locked the Wheeler and Callahan investigation files away in his own office. A few days later, John Connolly complained at length, saying that there was no reason for him to be denied access to the Wheeler and Callahan murder files.

Two institutional problems within the FBI worked to Bulger and Flemmi's advantage. While some agents, such as Montanari and Brunnick, were investigating criminals such as Bulger and Flemmi for serious violent crimes, other agents, such as Callahan, strove to protect and sometimes even bolster the same criminals if they were Top Echelon informants. Second, even though the attorney general's informant guidelines provided that "serious acts of violence" had to be reported either to the attorney general or to local authorities, this was rarely done. Such lapses allowed Bulger and Flemmi to simply slip through the cracks — with a significant boost from their pet agent John Connolly, who became something of a folk hero at the Boston FBI office due to his successes in Mafia wiretaps. He exploited his reputation in cultivating younger agents, particularly those who potentially might have targeted Bulger and Flemmi for investigation.[9]

Connolly treated Bulger and Flemmi as friends and recommended that other agents handling informants do likewise. He even took his supervisor, James Ring, to a Flemmi family dinner. Billy Bulger briefly attended the dinner as well, as he lived next door to Flemmi's parents. Ring asked Connolly not to socialize with gangsters again, but otherwise did nothing.

Between 1982 and 1985, agent John Morris accepted some $7,000 from Bulger and Flemmi. Usually, he received the bribes shortly after the Winter Hill leaders received information useful in their efforts to avoid prosecution and eliminate their enemies. The first $1,000 was handed to Morris's girlfriend and secretary shortly after Bulger and Flemmi received confirmation that Halloran was informing on them.[10]

The problem, of course, was that the most useful Top Echelon informants such as Bulger and Flemmi were involved in the very "serious acts of violence" that local agents were required to report. Yet, as H. Paul Rico readily acknowledged years later during a Congressional hearing, "people at all levels of the FBI" recognized that the organization had knowingly recruited murderers as informants.[11] Former Boston agents James Ring and John Morris didn't agree on much else during the hearing aside from the fact that the general FBI informant guidelines were totally incompatible with the TEPIC program.

In January 1995, Connolly, Bulger, and Flemmi were charged with racketeering, conspiracy, and obstruction of justice. Five and a half years later, in September 2000, Bulger and Flemmi were named in federal indictments charging them with eighteen murders. Six months later, Tulsa District Attorney Tim Harris filed parallel murder charges against

Bulger and Flemmi but declined at that time to charge H. Paul Rico.[12]

Once John Martorano decided to testify against his old bosses in 1999, Assistant District Attorney Jerry Truster of Tulsa gathered prosecutors from several jurisdictions at Cotton-Eyed Joe's Barbecue near Tulsa and cajoled them all into concurring that Martorano would get twelve and a half years in prison for twenty murders, more victims than Charles Manson, the Boston Strangler, and Richard Speck combined, although several DAs believed that Martorano deserved a heavier sentence.

Homicide detectives and other investigators from the same jurisdictions had not gotten along nearly so well. A few months before Truster's meeting at the barbecue joint, Tulsa homicide detective Mike Huff and eventual Massachusetts state police superintendent Thomas J. Foley nearly went to fists at Jim's Fish Shanty in Southie, a few steps away from where Brian Halloran had been shot in 1982. Foley had, in colorful language, claimed that Huff had messed up the Wheeler case. Mike Huff had had more than enough of the Boston Irish.

An Adventurous Life

Huff's father was a post office worker who sometimes had a second job to support his four children. His dad had urged him from adolescence to become a lawyer. Mike's dad also urged him to "live an adventurous life." Mike lived his father's dream for adventure through his work as a homicide investigator, following up leads wherever they might go. He was even in several gunfights, all unrelated to the Wheeler case.

As the years rolled by, the Wheeler case came to dominate everything in Huff's life. One Oklahoma Bureau of Investigation agent had convinced Huff that his phones at home and the office were tapped.

By the time Mike and his father spent their last evening together, Huff's dad had reconciled himself to Huff's passion for the thing he did well: chasing the bad guys. As Mike described a high-profile case he was pursuing, his dad encouraged Mike to do just what he'd been doing all those years since the Wheeler murder and "see it through."

Although he has no direct proof, Huff thinks he may have been responsible for the *Boston Herald* story "Gay Blade," in which Bulger's possible bi-sexuality was reported. It was Huff's reward poster that noted that Bulger had bad breath "that would knock you down." When asked whether Stephen Flemmi was Bulger's under boss, Huff opined that Bulger and Flemmi were equals. "Flemmi is his own man," Huff said, "I still get Christmas cards from him."

Getting Rid of Baggage

Despite having the local FBI office in his pocket, Steve Flemmi had other problems. His girlfriend, Debra Davis, a striking blonde in her twenties, was growing tired of their relationship. The two of them had been together for the better part of a decade by late 1981, but Debra was not Stevie's only conquest. Stevie was eyeing Debra's younger sister Michelle, whom he likened to Ava Gardner. She was only thirteen. Debra started dating a Mexican man, to Stevie's intense anger. Stevie had already reportedly shot one young man who had flirted with her in the back of the head.[13]

More important than his jealousy, though, she knew that Stevie was an FBI informant. Stevie and Whitey decided that Debra had to go. Jealousy aside, old times meant nothing, and, aside from Stevie's bruised ego, Debra had learned a lot about the FBI informant—she knew too much to go wandering off.

So, one September day in 1981, Stevie brought Debra to his parents' house while they were away. There, Whitey

Debra Davis. (Courtesy Polaris Images)

strangled her while Stevie watched, and then both went to work to cover their tracks. They methodically cut off her fingers and toes to eliminate any chance of identification, wrapped her stripped corpse in a sheet of plastic, and buried her in a marsh by the Neponset River. It was the same anonymous graveyard that held the body of hoodlum Tommy King, who'd been killed and planted there six years earlier, on November 5, 1975.

Even though he helped Whitey wipe out Paulie McGonagle in November 1974, Whitey never trusted Tommy King. Worse yet, Whitey and King got into a fight that King won. Howie Winter approved the hit, but Whitey was patient in carrying out his revenge. First, he had to convince King to trust him, so Whitey told him that the late Eddie Connors, killed on June 12, 1975, had a friend who was making noises about avenging the death of his pal Eddie.

It was all invention, but King bought it. The supposed target was Alan "Suitcase" Fidler, a real hoodlum. Whitey told King that he was part of the assassination team along with Flemmi and Martorano. As usual, everybody was given a .38 pistol in a paper bag — but King, not the brightest rooster in the coop, didn't check his revolver. If he had, he would have discovered that it wasn't loaded. The other three weapons were. As the four sat in the car, Martorano shot King in the back of the head, having thoughtfully given him the front seat.

Then it was off to Whitey's favorite marsh along the Neponset River, where the men unceremoniously ushered King to his final rest. One source remembered that whenever Whitey drove past the site of that anonymous grave, he would say, "Tip your hat to Tommy."[14]

King's best friend, Buddy Leonard, had grown up a neighbor of Whitey and Billy Bulger. When sober, Leonard was a tough guy too, and there was always the chance that he would have come looking for whoever had made King disappear. Killing Leonard might also confuse those investigating Tommy King's disappearance. And so, after King was shot, the three remaining men snagged Leonard in the early hours of November 6, 1975, outside a bar in Southie. He was drunk as usual, so it was easy. They pushed him into a car stolen from the recently departed King and then shot him. Nothing came of public and police curiosity about how Leonard ended up dead in his best friend's car; King became just one more casualty of the gang wars.

The Top of the Heap

By 1978, an increasing number of Boston area gangsters were looking for a way out. One was Fat Tony Ciulla, an ace horse-race fixer, who had been sold out by one of his crooked jockeys. Fat Tony talked at length to federal prosecutors, and then he told his story to *Sports Illustrated*. The magazine promptly published Fat Tony's profile in November 1978. Bulger, Flemmi, Howie Winter, and John Martorano were all mentioned in the article.[15]

Although Fat Tony hesitated to name names in open court, when a tough judge ordered him to testify, it seemed that Bulger and Flemmi were in for it. But then, ever-faithful John Connolly intervened. Whitey had shelled out lots of money over the years, so much that the FBI crook often left government paychecks un-cashed in his desk drawer for months.[16] Connolly and John Morris, who also took money from Whitey, went to the top in the FBI, to Jeremiah O'Sullivan, boss of the organized crime Strike Force.

O'Sullivan had no reason to disbelieve Connolly when he said that the Bureau needed both Bulger and Flemmi as informants in the campaign against the mafia. In fact, it was probably true. Even then, a plan was afoot to plant a bug in Mafia headquarters. In those desperate times, information was everything, and Bulger and Flemmi became unindicted co-conspirators, while the rest of the Winter Hill leadership found themselves in dire straits. After all, Bulger and Flemmi had the means to help with the biggest Mafia prosecutions in the Boston FBI district in 1978, at a time when "the Mafia was the Justice Department's highest priority."[17]

It had been a long road up from the ranks from the lowly beginnings as a hired gun, an enforcer, and an errand boy for other people. But when Howie Winter went to prison in 1979, Whitey found himself at the top of the heap. He also discovered, however, that it was harder to stay on top than it had appeared.

Martorano went to Florida, where he laid low for the next sixteen years (when he wasn't killing people), regularly supplied with as much as $1 million of Bulger's money.

Meanwhile, back in Massachusetts, in October 1979, James "Jimmy the Bear" Flemmi, Steve Flemmi's brother, died in prison of a drug overdose while serving eleven to eighteen years for attempted murder. He had turned a weekend furlough into three years on the lam but was recaptured and sent back; he released himself early through suicide.

That same year, Stevie's mother was mugged again, and Stevie asked Whitey to help move her to a "better" neighborhood. Whitey recommended a charming, vacant house complete with a white picket fence, right next door to his brother Billy. Whitey could meet there with Flemmi, their FBI contacts, and Billy. There was even a handy porch on which to store weaponry and anything else best not carried in public.

Eventually, Whitey felt that nobody could oppose or cross him without getting payback. As the Irish gangs got deeper and deeper into the drug trade, usually providing protection rather than the products themselves, more and more people seemed to be obstacles, hostile, or insulting. One such man was Joe Murray. In 1983, Joe was running a full-scale illicit drug warehouse in South Boston. Joe's error was his failure to pay protection money to Whitey, and sure enough, Joe was raided on a tip. The raid collected fifteen tons of marijuana and cost Joe a mint.

Whitey then offered Joe his protection, which included advance warning of future police raids on Joe's operation. All it cost Joe was a one-time payment of $80,000 and a partnership with Bulger. "Partnership" in this case meant that Bulger received half of the income from Murray's drug business but did none of the work. Joe bought it. He didn't have much choice.[18]

Of course, Joe didn't forget how he became "partners" with Bulger. In a 1989 conversation with FBI supervisor Ed Quinn, Murray offered to implicate Bulger and Flemmi in four "unsolved" murders. He also offered to testify that FBI agents John Connolly and John Newton were selling information on government investigations to Bulger and Flemmi.

Curiously, Quinn did not pursue the lead, but former *Boston Herald* journalist Ralph Ranalli chased it full bore after hearing several FBI agents at a retirement party joke about how Whitey Bulger was living in the basement of Connolly's suburban Boston home.[19] Ranalli later wrote a book about the FBI's secret partnership with the mob.

In the early 1980s, South Boston was connected to the tony downtown financial district by a creaky, rusted bridge. Although now somewhat gentrified, in the early 1980s Southie sported a dark, ominous waterfront featuring smelly fish-processing plants, down-on-their-luck shipyards, and second-rate seafood restaurants catering to tourists who found themselves in what later became the "Seaport District."

It was there that luck ran out for Edward Brian Halloran and his unlucky friend Michael Donahue on May 11, 1982. Donahue was the son of a cop, and Halloran's brother Barry also wore a badge, but that didn't do either of them any good that evening.

Brian Halloran was as cold a killer as Winter Hill ever

produced, maybe even colder than Martorano. Whitey called him "Balloonhead" because Brian's head was so disproportionately large compared with the rest of his body.

On one particular occasion, Halloran was driving a car with another gang member riding shotgun. There were two men in the back seat, and Halloran's assignment was to kill one of them. The two back-seat passengers thought that they were going out to have a drink or two. All was peaceful until Halloran stopped for a red light, turned in the driver's seat, and shot one of the passengers, spattering the interior of the car with blood. Brian's running mate in the front seat whispered that he'd shot the wrong man. "Now we're in the shit," the man muttered, but Brian wasn't bothered. He simply turned in the seat and shot the survivor. "Now we're out of the shit," he said.

Halloran had serious trouble with drugs and booze. He was a very loose cannon at the best of times and an immediate danger to Bulger, Flemmi, and Callahan. According to Flemmi's own account, Whitey Bulger, Flemmi, and John Callahan had offered Halloran the Roger Wheeler assassination and had given him $20,000 as a down payment. Halloran's efforts to join the Federal Witness Protection Program came to nothing. Bulger and Flemmi's two principal FBI sponsors convinced New England Organized Crime Task Force chief Jeremiah O'Sullivan that Halloran, a known cocaine addict, was too unstable to be trusted. They pointed out that Halloran was known within Winter Hill as a screw-up.

Assuming that Bulger and Flemmi were involved — which was a question in and of itself — special agent John Connolly and supervisory special agent John Morris asked themselves why would they have trusted Halloran with such a high-profile assassination. Besides, Bulger and Flemmi were important to the FBI's all-consuming case against the New England Mafia, which was a higher priority for the bureau than the Wheeler assassination.

Yes, Halloran publicly exposing Bulger and Flemmi as Top Echelon informants could jeopardize everything.

Neither Whitey Bulger nor his FBI partners would put up indefinitely with a walking liability such as Halloran. Halloran was also trouble for FBI agents Morris and Connolly, as he may have known about Bulger's payments. A case against the New England Italian-American Mafia head Jerry Angiulo and his *consigliere* Larry Zannino, based in part on information developed through Bulger and Flemmi, was nearing formal indictment.[20]

In 1977, Bulger and Flemmi had reconnoitered the 98 Prince Street headquarters that Angiulo and Zannino used to discuss Mafia business, identifying the numbers and locations of doors and alarms that would have to be compromised installing FBI surveillance equipment.

Whitey floated a rumor that Brian was an informer, and multiple attempts were made on his life. Brian and his friend Michael Donohue, who most sources say had nothing to do with the rackets, were blown away by a murder team in a special hit car, sporting a hot engine and a projector to spray oil on the street behind it to discourage pursuers.

Donahue was killed instantly by a bullet in the back of his head. When a police officer asked Halloran, dying, who had shot him, he named Jimmy Flynn, not realizing that Bulger had worn a disguise resembling Flynn.[21] Later, Flynn was tried and acquitted of all charges and went on to portray a judge in the film *Good Will Hunting*.

For a while, Whitey remained the boss of the Winter Hill gang. A few months before Halloran's death, Morris had told Connolly Halloran's story about being offered the Roger Wheeler hit. And after Halloran was murdered, since Callahan had admitted that he had passed news of the Halloran leak to Bulger and Flemmi, Morris "had few doubts about who had done it."[22]

The day after Halloran was murdered, Flemmi offered the FBI a ready, easily digestible explanation for the killing, designed to deflect attention away from Whitey Bulger and himself, claiming ". . . the wise guys in Charlestown, rather than Winter Hill or South Boston, supposedly heard that Halloran was going to cooperate with the law."[23]

Since Morris was then the FBI Organized Crime Squad supervisor in Boston and Connolly's supervisor, he had a major dilemma on his hands. Operating by the book would mean revealing what Connolly had done, but at the expense of violating two unspoken cardinal rules. First, agents were to never embarrass the Bureau, and second, in that place and time, the FBI placed destruction of the Italian-American Mafia above all other considerations. So Morris simply ignored what happened. A few months later, he had John Connolly deliver $1,000 in an envelope to Morris's secretary and girlfriend Debbie Noseworthy so that she could relieve his boredom at an FBI training site south of Savannah. Connolly told her that it was Morris's own money, but the cash actually had come from Whitey Bulger.[24]

Had Halloran made up the story about being offered the Wheeler contract? Or had Bulger and Flemmi planned to use Halloran for the assassination and then kill him too, as had happened with Eddie Connors? When Ed Quinn succeeded Morris as Boston FBI Organized Crime Unit supervisor, he interviewed Joe Murray on September 22, 1988. Murray suggested that Bulger and Flemmi indeed had intended to use Halloran for the Wheeler assassination and then kill him, too, but the Murray information was treated as unsubstantiated and omitted from the FBI file-indexing system, thus making the revelation virtually invisible to the field agents charged with investigating the Wheeler and Halloran murders in 1989.

Later, United States magistrate judge Mark Wolf concluded that keeping Bulger and Flemmi as Top Echelon informants was more important to the FBI than prosecuting them. And, according to one Boston-area investigative reporter who researched the issue exhaustively, this was not merely a decision by several rogue agents in Boston. "When faced with either pursuing prosecutions of its own Top Echelon Informants or protecting them, the FBI as an agency chose to protect them."[25]

Whitey's virtually unlimited access to knowledge about the criminal world increased his power — and his income. When it suited him, he sold out denizens of the crime world, primarily those of the Italian Mafia. Others he simply shook down, much as he had treated Joe Murray and as he tried to do with an oily-haired, bulbous-nosed master burglar named Arthur "Bucky" Barrett.

Bucky owned a bar in Boston called Rascal's, but on the side he was a highly accomplished safe cracker. In May 1980, exactly a year before Roger Wheeler was assassinated, he had been part of the gang that tunneled into the Depositors Trust Bank over the course of one weekend and robbed hundreds of safety deposit boxes. Bucky's crew had included several local law officers, including a Metropolitan Police captain and a Medford, Massachusetts, police lieutenant. Yet, despite this support from local law enforcement, Bucky had a major problem.

Many of those boxes were owned by the Mafia or Irish gang members and contained huge sums of cash; after all, what the IRS didn't know about wasn't taxable. The tunneling crew's take was enormous, and news of it immediately drew the attention of the king of Winter Hill. Worse yet, Bucky had not consulted Whitey before doing the job. Once Whitey learned of Bucky's involvement, he had FBI agent Morris warn Bucky that Whitey was offended. Bucky contacted his own sponsors in the police in return — some of whom were also involved in the bank tunnel robbery — and forced Whitey to back off.

Whitey had a long memory for anybody who bucked him, and he was a patient man. Three years later, in August 1983, Bucky was lured to a house in Southie by an offer to fence some non-existent diamonds. There, he was knocked around and bullied both for money and for information, especially regarding Joe Murray. Bucky conducted a telephone marathon with his friends and relatives for a few thousand, and at the end of a long, weary day Whitey gave him the usual bullet in the back of the head.

Stevie Flemmi pulled out most of Bucky's teeth with a pair of pliers. Then, they dug a grave in the basement and interred Bucky without benefit of clergy and covered in lime to make him disappear faster.

The Valhalla Caper

Like many of the Boston Irish, Whitey Bulger—and Stevie Flemmi, although he was in no way Irish—had a soft spot for the Irish Republican Army. So did hefty, thick-necked John McIntyre, who told the Drug Enforcement Agency (DEA) just enough about the involvement of Bulger and Flemmi in one gun-running operation to get himself killed. Bulger's support for the IRA had intensified once he had become an FBI informant, and, in 1987, he obtained Irish citizenship.[26]

McIntyre crewed on the seventy-seven-foot *Valhalla*, which had been filled to the decks with the largest shipment of munitions ever shipped from the United States to the IRA. A smaller vessel, used to convey the arms and munitions from the sea into port, ran straight into the waiting net of the authorities. The *Valhalla* itself was impounded the minute it entered United States waters.

After trying to climb up a drainpipe into his ex-wife's second story apartment and being arrested on old charges, McIntyre told the DEA about a certain thirty-six-ton marijuana shipment headed into Boston Harbor, costing Bulger and Flemmi about $1 million in protection money. Naturally, the DEA told their FBI counterparts about McIntyre, and word found its way to John Connolly.

On November 30, 1984, McIntyre attended a party, carrying a case of beer with him. He soon found himself looking into the cold eyes of Whitey Bulger. After six hours of verbal interrogation, Bulger learned that John McIntyre had not snitched out the *Valhalla* shipment. Years later, the public learned that the Irish lost the *Valhalla* thanks to an informant in IRA's leadership named Sean O'Callaghan.

The loss of the marijuana shipment, however, was McIntyre's fault, and that was enough for one of Whitey's death sentences. The party ended in the basement, where Bulger did his very best to strangle the thick-necked man. Exasperated after a few minutes of effort, Bulger asked, "Do you just want a bullet in the head?"

"Yes, please," said McIntyre, and so it was.

It Was Business, Not Personal

Soon afterwards, in 1985, Whitey helped Stevie Flemmi kill Deborah Hussey, Stevie's step-daughter through his common-law wife, Marion Hussey. Deborah was nothing if not precocious. She had been intimately involved with Flemmi since she was fifteen years old, and as she grew older, he showered her with presents, including a Jaguar and her own apartment. By age seventeen, Deborah had dropped out of high school and progressed from bar waitress to stripper.

One day, she threw a memorable tantrum in front of her mother, during which she accused Stevie of molesting her as a child. Deborah's mother responded by throwing Flemmi out of the house, which he owned.

Because Deborah knew about Flemmi's FBI informant status, she could not be simply relied on to keep quiet. Whitey did his usual job of strangling Deborah in early 1985. Stevie finished the job with a rope and a stick. The men chopped off her fingers and toes and pulled her teeth in

Deborah Hussey. (Courtesy author's collection)

order to prevent any identification of the body. She received a basement grave next to Bucky Barrett. Both bodies were dug up later and moved to a spot near Florian Hall not far from Tenean Beach in Dorchester.[2] During the reinterment, a passing car had slowed down to look at the men but did not stop. Whitey grew angry because his colleagues hadn't killed the passing driver to ensure there were no witnesses. That anger was a glimpse into a very dark soul.

Once Whitey and his partner, Flemmi, were in full control of the Winter Hill gang in late 1979, the money began to roll in. As late as 1980, one rival said that Whitey didn't have two nickels to rub together, but as king of the hill, he had the respect that every criminal craved. However, there were clouds on their horizon—the human damage they had left behind on their road to power would not vanish so easily.

With the change in management, Howie Winter's often tolerant ways of business were over. Whitey believed in ruling with an iron fist, his way or the highway. With Flemmi as brutal as Whitey himself and their chief assassin John Martorano on the prowl, the members of the gang did exactly as they were told. Whitey briefly ran the show from the Marshall Motors garage in Somerville, which had been Winter Hill headquarters since the Eisenhower years. He conducted business and administered discipline in the back office. Today, the Marshall Motors building is a church.

Bulger moved their headquarters into Boston proper in early 1980.[28] They settled on a West End garage on Lancaster Street, a quicker commute from South Boston than Somerville. Still, shades of the old days haunted them—including their old Irish Gang War nemesis George McLaughlin, who spent his weekend prison furloughs in Charlestown, getting close to a whole new generation of gangsters. George had not forgotten about the Irish war; in particular, he hugged the memory of his kin, Bernie and Punchy, who had been victims of Whitey and his associates.

Georgie McLaughlin raised twenty-four-year-old Steve Hughes Jr. as his protégé. Hughes's father had been killed by Flemmi back in 1966. Hughes, who was already on parole for bank robbery, was a clear danger to Whitey. He was picked off in January 1980 with a rifle from a housetop as he sat in a car with his wife and child, dead before his own criminal career really had even started.[29] The FBI immediately learned about the murder, but the whole matter simply disappeared from official view.

Once the new Winter Hill garage headquarters was discovered, the Feds bugged it. Audio tapes recorded Whitey screaming at new henchman Nicky Femia not to "bring such s---" as French fries into his place, although Whitey denied this years later. Femia had been a suspect in many murders, but Whitey's in-house FBI agent John Connolly had helpfully filed reports absolving him of any responsibility. Law enforcement didn't learn much else because Whitey simply stopped using bugged premises or bugged phones, again warned off by Connolly.

One more housekeeping problem for Whitey emerged two years after the move to the Lancaster Street garage. Like Howie Winter before him, Whitey considered himself to be all-powerful in his criminal domain. That meant that nobody got murdered or knocked around as a matter of gang business unless Whitey blessed it in advance.

That rule got Louie Latif into trouble. Latif was a bookkeeper who began expanding into the drug business. He flamboyantly appeared in the disco movie *Saturday Night Fever*, sporting super-long sideburns, a droopy mustache, and showy shirts. Latif had murdered a couple of people without clearing the killings first, which of course aroused Whitey's ire. But that wasn't what got Latif killed. John Connolly overheard a defense lawyer telling a friend that Latif was about to inform on Bulger and Flemmi.[30] Latif also had offered his services as a police informant for the state in Connolly's presence, who relayed the information to Whitey.

In April 1980, Louie Latif was led to the slaughter by none other than Brian Halloran, out of prison and back into booze and cocaine.[31] Halloran led Latif into a trap, where Whitey did the job himself. Latif ended up dead of acute ice pick and bullet in the trunk of his own car, parked in front of a laundromat owned by a Mafia soldier to whom Whitey wanted to send a message.[32] Whitey was still kingpin of his crooked little domain, but there were cracks forming in the walls.

When one of Latif's daughters approached Connolly for help obtaining proof of death so that the family could claim his insurance, the FBI man leveled with her. "Honey, your father's dead. But don't worry. They got him drunk first."[33] Connolly did help the family break the insurance settlement loose, but his statement was a virtual admission that he was privy to Winter Hill crimes.

Late in the summer of 1988, a stranger sidled up to Paul

Corsetti, a reporter for the *Boston Herald,* out on the prowl at a bar in the Faneuil Hall Marketplace at 1 a.m. "I'm Whitey Bulger, m----- f-----, and I f-----' kill people for a living." That vague threat, uttered shortly after Corsetti began writing an article about the murder of Louis Latif, captured his immediate attention. Whitey wasn't that concerned about the murder accusation. His real beef was the rumor that Corsetti was going to tie him to IRA weapons buyers and drag his brother Billy Bulger into the story. Corsetti was no hero — he wrote a toned-down article and let the dirt lie. No doubt the reporter was relieved when a Mafia acquaintance told him that his story was "no problem."[34]

Chapter 7
Wollaston Beach

There was a full moon on the night of September 18, 1975, in Quincy, where FBI agent John Connolly waited two hours for Whitey Bulger — at least, that's how he told the story. He had a proposition to make. Whitey slipped into the front seat of Connolly's car before he even knew it.

About a month earlier, a dispute between North End Patriarca crime family boss Jerry Angiulo and the Winter Hill gang erupted over vending machines in predominately Irish Somerville, Charlestown, and South Boston. The dispute was about to erupt, and Connolly wanted to strike a deal.

Connolly and Bulger hadn't met for years, although Whitey's younger brother Billy had been a guidance counselor of sorts for Connolly, urging him to work his way through college and find a career. Later, after Connolly became an FBI agent, Billy asked Connolly to "keep my brother out of trouble."

The Paramount Informant

They quickly got down to business. Connolly claimed that Angiulo was informing on Winter Hill to take out the competition. "You can't survive without friends in law enforcement," Whitey observed. That's exactly why Connolly arranged this meeting through a mutual friend. "Why don't you use us [the FBI] to do what they're doing to you? Fight fire with fire." Then he leaned closer and said, "You take out a Mafia family and you'd be the talk of the country."

Whitey said he'd think about it, but, as a point of pride, added, "I'm a big boy. I chose this business." With that, he vanished.

Two weeks later, they met again at Wollaston Beach. Whitey made a counteroffer of sorts. "I'm no f------ informant," he said, "I'm the *liaison* for Winter Hill. We're not hurting any of our friends." Finally, any discussion of the Irish Republican Army was "off the table." Whitey's afterthought as he closed the car door: his brother couldn't know.[1]

And so, Whitey joined his Winter Hill partner Stevie Flemmi as an informant for the FBI, having served the agency in that capacity briefly four years before.[2] The order to make Bulger a top echelon informant in 1971 is said to have come from the office of J. Edgar Hoover himself, even though Bulger's informant file was closed a short time later by Agent Dennis Condon. One uncorroborated source asserts that FBI agent H. Paul Rico followed Bulger to a gay bar and used Whitey's involvement there as blackmail to force him into ratting out his colleagues.

Whitey probably had few qualms about joining Flemmi as a Top Echelon informant. Whitey was perfectly willing to sell out not only *Mafiosi* but also any number of his Irish gang members to law enforcement and the FBI. Although there's nothing more disgraceful in the eyes of most professional criminals than an informer, such loyalty was sometimes quickly overcome when self-interest entered the picture. So it was with Whitey Bulger.

Bulger and Flemmi eventually turned themselves into two of the most poisonous and successful traitors of all time. From within an outlaw society in which everybody paid at least lip service to the quixotic notion of loyalty unto death, they gave up man after man to the Feds.

Their plan had nothing to do with loyalty, fear, or revenge. Instead, it had everything do with getting government immunity for their own crimes so they could advance in the rackets any way they chose, included serial murders.

The Top Echelon Informant Program plan began in 1961, ostensibly at least, as a praiseworthy campaign by the FBI to undermine the Mafia and bring down its primary leaders. J. Edgar Hoover seems to have been willing to use almost any instrument to get convictions of some veteran *Mafiosi;* Bulger and, more frequently, Flemmi were mines of information, and Hoover praised their handlers accordingly.

In the mid-1970s, having friends in the FBI paid well. Whitey knew that a little clout in government could save a man a world of trouble, even as he watched his brother Billy progress up the Massachusetts political ladder. At least, it paid very well to operate as a protected, or paramount, informant as long as agents without conscience did the protecting.

Two agents stood out among the rest, two men so focused on Director Hoover's goals and their careers that they did not care in the least of what Whitey and Flemmi were guilty, as long as the agents got the glory of mafia arrests and convictions. John Connolly and H. Paul Rico, many law enforcement officers believed, were willing to overlook murder to obtain the information Hoover wanted. The *Tulsa World* called this incestuous arrangement "the cozy relationship between the FBI's organized crime unit and murderous underworld informants in Boston in the 1960s and 1970s."[3]

Conflict emerged in the Boston FBI office immediately after Wheeler's murder in 1981. Both Mike Huff and Wheeler's sons Larry and David knew intuitively that their father's death was somehow related to World Jai Alai. FBI agent John Morris followed the appropriate procedures, dispatching John Connolly to interview Callahan, who claimed he had nothing to do with Winter Hill, just as Whitey and Flemmi denied any such relationship. Morris took his first bribe, a case of fine wine, shortly thereafter.

When Huff disregarded normal protocol and contacted John Connolly in Boston personally, Connolly would only say "that his job was to take down the [Mafia], not investigate his Irish."[4]

"I know who killed Roger Wheeler,," Brian Halloran told FBI agents Leo Brunnick and Gerry Montanari three days after Christmas in 1981. Halloran wasn't just being a good citizen. He was implicated in the early-morning murder of a drug dealer named George Pappas in October 1981 at a greasy spoon in Boston's Chinatown called the Four Seasons.[5]

Halloran had gone there with Jackie Salemme to remind Pappas that he owed the Mafia some tribute money. Halloran had every reason to fear that the Pappas murder would be pinned on him or, worse yet, that either Winter Hill or the Mafia would kill Halloran to keep his mouth shut.

He claimed that a few months earlier, in the spring of 1981, his friend John Callahan had invited him to Callahan's office overlooking the Boston Harbor for drinks. When he arrived, Halloran found that Whitey Bulger and Steve Flemmi were there too. Callahan did the talking, saying that this guy in Tulsa named Roger Wheeler had to be killed before he discovered that Callahan had been skimming money from World Jai Alai.

Much to everyone's surprise, Halloran had asked if there was some other way to deal with Wheeler. Whitey sneered at him, the meeting broke up, and Callahan said that he would be in touch. Within two weeks, according to Halloran, Callahan paid him $20,000 to forget about Wheeler.[6]

Of course, Montanari and Brunnick reported this to Morris, who told Whitey and Flemmi, sealing Halloran's fate.

Some have said Halloran identified Jimmy Flynn as his killer because of Whitey's disguise, consisting of blonde hair and a mustache.[7] Later, after Whitey described killing Halloran, Steve lamented, "I wish I was there."[8]

After FBI agent John Morris guzzled a six-pack of his favorite beer, courtesy of Whitey, Morris alerted the mob boss that an agent tailing Halloran on a drug case got the license plate on the "tow truck," Whitey's customized getaway car, which he quickly dismantled. "Thank God for Beck's [beer]," Whitey said later.[9]

Two weeks after the May 1982 Halloran hit, with FBI field agents from Oklahoma City, Boston, and Miami crowded around a small conference room, Washington DC-based organized crime section chief Sean McWeeney emphasized that Whitey and Steve "were extremely valuable assets" in the war against the Mafia. More specifically, the Washington FBI office had every practical reason to protect these key informants in the developing case against New England Mafia boss Jerry Angiulo.[10]

Halloran's Wake

Mike Huff was not surprised when Halloran turned up dead. About a year after the Wheeler murder, Stanley Glanz, then serving as chief of detectives with the Tulsa Police Department, called in all homicide detectives citywide for an early morning meeting. Their mission was to canvas hotels on the interstate near Southern Hills Country Club looking for anything they could find on Winter Hill gang assassin John Martorano. The source was a small-time associate of the Winter Hill gang named Brian Halloran.

Later that year, in 1982, as Huff walked into his house, the phone rang. It was about this same Brian Halloran. Huff had been looking for Halloran but couldn't find him, as Halloran had been living on Cape Cod at the government's expense while his application for the Federal Witness Protection Program was reviewed.

Brian "Balloonhead" Halloran had been mentioned to Tulsa detectives in July 1981, a mere two months after the Wheeler murder, but when Stanley Glanz called the meeting some ten months later, Huff had not yet established a relationship with the Massachusetts State Police.

The "Staties" were hesitant to use their own phones in conversations with Tulsa Police because of surveillance concerns. "You had to get on a plane, travel halfway across the country and hope you could catch someone in the office and hope you could get them to trust you, all in a matter of minutes," Huff recalled in an interview. Eventually, Huff developed a relationship with the Connecticut State Police, professionals who suspected from the beginning of the Wheeler investigation (if not before) that Rico was crooked. By July 1982, Huff believed he had his arms around enough information to meet with the Massachusetts State Police.

Huff's goal was to obtain enough evidence to confront Halloran. "All I brought [to the investigation] was energy," he recalled in an April 2013 interview, recognizing his relative inexperience at the time. "I hadn't been on the job long enough to be scared of anybody." Fortunately, his long-experienced partner Dick Bishop "cleaned up" after Huff "when he pissed people off."

Huff would start at noon, four hours before his shift began, devoting some five hours per day to the Wheeler case. He recalled that, to some degree, he was a "social director" focused on developing relationships with Connecticut and Massachusetts law enforcement to get leads. But even then there was a problem. Huff sometimes found himself, "flying halfway across the country for a two-page report" that the state police "guarded like a piece of gold" since, working under the shadow of Billy Bulger's political and familial connections, they didn't want their investigation to haunt their careers. "Everyone was very vulnerable," Huff recalled, "Nobody sees it for the intensity which it required."

Did Wheeler know that he was in danger? Not until the last, in Huff's view. Shortly before he died, Wheeler and his chief pilot had attended a seminar on avoiding kidnapping.

Wheeler had also tried to put Rico on a polygraph, but Rico had refused. About two weeks before he was killed, while Wheeler and his son David were deep-sea fishing near Miami, Wheeler told David that he wanted to fire Donovan despite his agreement with First National Bank of Boston, but Donovan was nowhere to be found.

Just until a few weeks before his death, Wheeler had thought that he was invincible. "What are they going to do, kill me?" he told one friend. He considered himself untouchable because World Jai Alai was an actual organization governed by state regulation. "This is a legitimate business," Wheeler reportedly said, "and I'm going to run it like one."

Why did Whitey Bulger agree to the Wheeler hit, despite his concerns that it "will never go away?" Huff theorizes that Bulger's motive for the Wheeler hit might have been control—the desire to eventually control World Jai Alai and everybody involved in it, just as Bulger had in the Winter Hill gang. One intriguing question about the murder is whether Bulger was collecting any of the WJA skim before Wheeler's assassination. More certainly, in Huff's view, Callahan and Rico were in on the scheme. One investigator has speculated that Donovan might have been in on it as well.

Years after Wheeler was assassinated, Huff learned that Joe McDonald had asked for his part of the World Jai Alai skim. Martorano contacted Flemmi, who dutifully arranged a meeting with Rico in Miami. However, Rico pulled Flemmi into a side conference. Flemmi returned and simply said, "There's nothing here," meaning that there would be no new skim.

Boston was a dirty old town in 1982, the heyday of the mob. One of the FBI's superstars was H. Paul Rico because of the cases he'd made against the Italian Mafia, La Cosa Nostra. Yet this was the expense of the truth and, in a few cases, crimes against the legal system, which let organized-crime figures be convicted of crimes in which they were not involved.

On one occasion, while he was following leads in Boston, Huff was followed by FBI agents who weren't difficult to spot. They were the ones "wearing white shirts and wingtip shoes, driving big cars with little hubcaps."

Huff soon found that there was no real police budget for investigative travel. His applications for travel to follow up on the Wheeler case in out-of-town trips had to be approved by the mayor of Tulsa. Some of the other homicide detectives resented these trips because they were working more than their share of routine murder cases so that Huff could follow up on flimsy leads that didn't lead to prompt results.

Callahan Must Go

John Connolly in effect ordered Callahan's death in the summer of 1982 when he told Whitey, "You're going to get a lot of heat on this." Connolly opined that Callahan would crack and tell all if confronted with his role in the Halloran murder.[11] Martorano, Callahan's longtime friend, would have to kill him.

It wasn't an easy sell, but, in the end, Whitey and Flemmi drove down to the LaGuardia Marriott in New York City to give Martorano the bad news. Since Martorano was still wanted in the Boston horse-race fixing indictments, he arrived at the hotel as Richard Aucoin. He was reluctant to kill a friend, but after a brief argument, Whitey asked one question: "Can he [Callahan] do twenty years?" Martorano had to admit that he couldn't.

Meanwhile, in Tulsa, Mike Huff pressed the Oklahoma City FBI office to push for an interview with Bulger and Flemmi. In April 1983, the Oklahoma-based FBI agents arranged one, but not before John Connolly planted a Bulger alibi in the FBI records.[12]

Seven months later, Gerry Montanari and FBI agent Brendan Cleary interviewed Whitey and Flemmi in the old Mullen gang clubhouse in South Boston, of all places. The previous year, Morris, now plied with cash, fine wines, and other bribes, had given John Connolly a performance rating that said his work "substantially exceeded superior performance" and was "truly exceptional."

By the time Callahan was killed, Bulger had come to regret the Wheeler, Halloran, Donohue, and Callahan killings and began to irreverently call them the "Holy Trinity."[13]

The Deborah Hussey killing in 1985 and sale of the house where Hussey, McIntyre, and Barrett were buried coincided with a new phase in Whitey's career. He was fifty-six years old and had transitioned from killing his adversaries to simply threatening them with death. In a sense, he was following his doctor's orders to "slow down," now that he was taking blood pressure medicine to deal with occasional arrhythmia. By this time, as Whitey's protégé Kevin Weeks later explained, "We didn't need to kill anyone anymore."[14]

Protected as he was by the FBI, Whitey now moved into serial extortion. Ray Slinger, a South Boston real estate agent who Whitey initially consulted in 1986 about possible investments, soon found himself agreeing to pony up $50,000 just to stay in business. After a call to the local FBI office, Slinger was let off the hook, but other extortion schemes helped Whitey pile up a large cash boodle.

The second half of the 1980s exposed Whitey to new public scrutiny. The *Boston Globe* revealed the relationship between him and Connolly in a September 1988 series of articles, much to Whitey's consternation. A presidential commission on organized crime described him as a bank robber, drug trafficker, and murderer. He was irate. "I'm no drug trafficker," Whitey asserted at a wedding.[15]

Eight years earlier, community organizers Dan and Nancy Yotts began to complain that Whitey and Billy Bulger were running South Boston. Billy monopolized all South Boston patronage jobs, the Yotts claimed, while Whitey permitted drug pushers and users to run amok. But after a few slashed tires and threatening phone calls, the Yotts moved elsewhere in late 1987.[16]

Two Ceremonies

The house in Medford, Massachusetts, was modest, but the occasion, momentous. On October 29, 1989, four men were to be inducted into the mafia. Neither the initiates nor the nine other men present knew it, but the FBI was listening in, compliments of Whitey and Flemmi, who had handed John Connolly exactly the informant he needed to cap his career, a snitch named Angelo "Sonny" Mercurio.

That one-hour ceremony, complete with whispered oaths of *omertà* (silence), pricked fingers, and burning of holy cards, produced twenty-one immediate arrests and important rebuttal evidence that could be used whenever criminal defense lawyers claimed that the Mafia did not exist. This evidence made Connolly the toast of the FBI, and FBI director William Sessions attended the press conference publicizing the Medford induction arrests.

Earlier in that decade, in the mid-1980s, Connolly had showed off Bulger and Flemmi to his old friend FBI agent Joe Pistone, whose career was dramatized in the film *Donnie Brasco*. Now at the summit of his career, Connolly planned to retire and write his own Brasco-esque memoirs. He accepted a cushy job as director of security at Boston Edison, a local power company.

July 1990 found Bulger and Flemmi in tall cotton. Bulger either won or acquired one sixth of a lottery ticket with a total payoff of $14.3 million. That put an additional $80,000 per month into his pocket. Years later, law enforcement concluded that Whitey had paid someone $700,000 interest for his share, but Weeks maintained that this story had been concocted to lessen Flemmi's irritation.

When Connolly retired from the FBI that December, Billy Bulger was one of the speakers at the ceremony. "John Connolly is the personification of loyalty," said Billy, "Not only to his friends and not only to the job he holds but to the highest principles. He's never forgotten them."[17]

With Connolly's retirement, Bulger and Flemmi retired too. Bulger stashed cash all over the country as well as in Dublin, London, and Montreal. Flemmi, on the other hand, invested in Boston-area real estate investments of about $1 million.[18] Neither the FBI nor the Department of Justice ever apologized to any of Bulger's victims' families.

Chapter 8

Turning Point

Billy Bulger ended his career in public service as president of the University of Massachusetts. His memoirs, published a few years later, waxed eloquent on his January 1996 appointment. "I see my decision as a change of venue, not in career. The music to which I refer in this book [*While the Music Lasts*] is the harmony that public service has brought to my life for the thirty-four years I have spent in the legislature. The music goes on, strange and clear and sweet as ever, in the challenge of leading the University of Massachusetts to the realization of its potential as one of the very best, as well as one of the biggest, universities in the nation. I can think of no greater public service I might perform."[1] That said, in just a few years, the university staff grew to accommodate ever larger numbers of ex-politicians and other friends of Billy, a practice then common in Massachusetts. One former state representative even found himself in the role of associate chancellor.

This happy situation was not to last. When knowledge of his brother's many crimes became public, Billy found himself testifying before a congressional committee on June 19, 2003. For a man with an illustrious career as a public speaker, he did not live up to his reputation. There were a lot of "I don't recalls" mixed in with a variety of "I don't remembers," much of it delivered haltingly, with a lot of "ums" and "ahs" thrown in. The classic orator perpetually pointing his right index finger at the audience was gone.

165

The committee smelled weakness and pushed Bulger even harder.

Once he had been granted immunity from prosecution, the Fifth Amendment was no longer a refuge for Billy. Committee members questioned many of his actions in the state senate, such as hiring political cronies and friends from South Boston. They asked some very hard questions about political favors and pushed particularly hard about his relationship with his brother Whitey. Billy fell back on euphemisms served up from a prepared statement, "I am particularly sorry to think that he may have been guilty of some of the horrible things of which he is accused."[2]

"I now recognize," he lamely said, "that I did not fully grasp the dimensions of his life . . . I still live in the hope that the worst of the charges against him will prove groundless. It is my hope . . ."

Few, if any, on the committee believed him. The pointed, embarrassing questions were bipartisan now. Committee chairman Dan Burton asked the most unanswerable question of all: "Mr. Bulger, what did you think your brother did for a living?"

Bulger's response told everybody listening just exactly what Billy Bulger was made of: "I had the feeling that he was, uh, in the business of gaming, and, uh, whatever. It was vague to me but I didn't think, uh, for a long while he had some jobs but, uh, ultimately it was clear that he was not, uh, um, being um, uh, you know, he wasn't doing what I'd like him to do."[3] His halting, unhelpful testimony did him no good at all, and there was nobody to throw him a line.

His friends in Massachusetts politics were unavailable. Gov. Michael Dukakis had long since left office. The new governor, Mitt Romney, made no secret of what he thought of Billy Bulger. Even so, Bulger thought he had enough protection from his loyal university trustees to be well safeguarded in his job, whatever the committee or the governor said or thought.

He was wrong. Three positions on the University of Massachusetts board of trustees became vacant in the fall of 2003. Governor Romney announced who his nominees would be: an astute and fearless columnist for the *Boston Herald*, the distinguished lawyer Alan Dershowitz, and a judge who had once referred to Billy as a "corrupt midget."

Bulger was astonished. "He wouldn't dare," he said. But Romney surely did. Two weeks after learning Romney's proposals, in September 2003, Billy resigned as the university president. In the end, his twenty honorary degrees did him little good. Ted Kennedy said that he was "saddened," and Bill Clinton called to express his regrets. Billy made the most of his departure, leaving with almost $1 million cash in settlement and a pension of more than $11,000 per month, the largest pension in the history of the state. His exodus from office was followed by the departure of several of his highly paid staffers.

Billy was gone, but he wasn't through. Back before the state retirement board, he demanded that his pension be increased another $32,000. He lost 5-0. On the same docket was Jackie Bulger, Billy and Whitey's brother, who shared Whitey's pattern baldness and Billy's preference for button-down shirts and khakis. Jackie demanded restoration of his own pension, a meager $44,000 per year. He argued on the ground that, even if he did commit a batch of felonies while a government employee, he was not indicted until after his resignation. The same board was profoundly underwhelmed by that argument and gave Jackie the same vote as Billy.

Billy's downfall did not happen overnight, however. The thirteen-year course of events was curious indeed.

Evil

James Bulger was a complex man.

On the surface, he appeared to be no more than a thug

Bulger plays cowboy. (Courtesy Polaris Images)

who especially liked his work, but there was a lot more to him. He was very able and intelligent and had a powerful sense of self-preservation. That instinct, together with an enormous lust for both power and money, drove him to commit vile deeds. Whitey also had unlimited capacity for cruelty. On the other hand, he was concerned about his health, given to juices, vitamins, healthy meals, and regular workouts.

One of the Southie toughs who had been his adversary, John "Red" Shea, told this story about him: Whitey and his shadow, Kevin Weeks, confronted Shea in 1985, demanding details about Tommy Connors, who Whitey said owed him money. Both Whitey and Weeks brandished Uzi submachine guns. Shea was alone and unarmed. He also was, according to his account, uncowed. He refused to say anything about Connors. When Whitey cocked the Uzi, Shea said, "I looked him right in the eyes. They are cold as ice." Of Connors, Shea told the men, "He's done nothing. Do what you gotta do."[4]

Whitey jacked a round into the Uzi, but, after a moment, he uncocked the weapon, smiled at Shea, and said, "It was a test, Red. You passed. You've got f----- b-- b----. You're loyal. You're one loyal f----- guy. Now you're with me." The next day, Whitey made him top dog in the gang's drug business.

For a while, Shea and Bulger got along. Once, when Shea was having trouble recovering some of his jewelry, Whitey stopped the jeweler in question on the street. "Do you know who I am?" Whitey asked. The jeweler said no, although he probably knew very well. Whitey began shouting, "I am f----- Whitey Bulger, that's who I am. I'll blow your f----- head off if you don't give my friend his stuff back, you understand that, you c--- s-----?" Shea says that the jeweler urinated in his pants from fear.

Whitey was also a teacher and mentor for the younger hoodlums, according to Shea. His rules for success were elementary. If you talk business, keep the radio on; don't wear flashy clothes; don't act in haste or anger; don't drive a conspicuous car; and don't give anybody anything to hold over you. He also had one unusual maxim: "Get your women a white car," Whitey advised, "so you can spot 'em."[5]

Shea ultimately did ten years of hard time for his part in the Winter Hill gang's crimes. He kept his mouth shut throughout, although he knew enough to buy himself a serious reduction in his sentence, maybe to escape prison altogether. Not so his mentor.

Breakthrough

Tom Foley only had one objective when he began running the special services section of the Massachusetts State Police in the fall of 1990. He focused all his resources on taking down Bulger and his partner Flemmi, employing a strategy that seasoned FBI agents rejected out of hand. Foley focused on identifying and turning disgruntled bookies. His primary target was Burton "Chico" Krantz, a major Boston bookie who was paying tribute to Bulger and Flemmi.

The key to the case was surveillance placed at Heller's, a Chelsea bar where bookies could cash checks nominally payable to then-famous sports stars such as the golfer Arnold Palmer or basketball player Bill Russell. The cash was doled out by Heller's bar cashier, Mike London, whom the state police had indicted and turned into an informant. Through London, they learned that Chico was not happy. From a Jewish family, he had grown up in Dorchester dodging Irish and Italian kids untutored in diversity; Chico considered the payments to Bulger and Flemmi wasted money.

Early in 1991, Foley's surveillance team followed money mule "Fat Vinnie" Roberto to Chico's door. The cops took some cash that Vinnie was delivering, parlayed that into a warrant for the search of Chico's house, and found keys to two safety deposit boxes in nearby banks. And so, when the state police grabbed $2 million out of those boxes, Chico wanted to make a deal. Still, he wasn't willing to inform on Bulger and Flemmi. "They'd kill me. They'd kill my family," Chico said, but changed his mind when Foley told him that his wife, Jacqui Krantz, was about to be indicted along with him.

At about 3 p.m. on December 23, 1994, John Connolly walked into the South Boston Liquor Mart. "Is the other guy around?" Connolly asked Kevin Weeks. Weeks and Connolly adjourned to the beer cooler, where the loud hum of refrigeration equipment made effective surveillance impossible. It was there that Connolly delivered the message. Federal indictments, developed by Tom Foley's task force, naming Bulger, Flemmi, and their sometime-ally Cadillac Frank Salemme, were imminent. FBI snitch Connolly had learned about it first hand from his long-time friend Dennis O'Callaghan, then the number two man in the Boston FBI office.

Within minutes, Bulger responded to Weeks's page, picked him up, and drove to the Neiman Marcus department store in Copley Square, where Teresa Stanley, Whitey's then-girlfriend, began to window shop as Weeks shared the news. "Let's go," Whitey yelled, just before telling her about his surprise. They were going on a long, long vacation. "You gotta get a hold of Stevie," Whitey said, back at the liquor store about an hour later. When Weeks did just that, Flemmi was inexplicably relaxed about the news. "My guy is right on top of everything," he assured Weeks, referring to Richard Schneiderhan, a state police officer who had been keeping Flemmi up to date on indictments for years.[6]

Flemmi was wrong. After he was arrested on the evening of Thursday, January 5, 1995, as state police officer Tommy Duffy gave Flemmi an earful about the fifty witnesses who were going to put him away, an FBI agent drew close and uttered a warning: "This thing of ours, it's not like it used to be. There's no more respect."

The FBI gradually increased the pace of the pursuit. A $250,000 reward was first offered in 1996, and Whitey was featured on *America's Most Wanted* in 1999, two years after an interagency federal task force was appointed.

The Wolf Decision

On September 19, 1999, US district judge Mark Wolf of Boston concluded a fifty-witness, eleven-month hearing by releasing a 661-page decision addressing Steve Flemmi's argument that all charges against him should be dropped because the FBI had given him immunity. While Judge Wolf rejected Flemmi's claim that he and Bulger had been granted immunity, the judge opined that the FBI had virtually created a partnership with the two, bottomed on "an antipathy for [La Cosa Nostra] a desire to profit criminally from its destruction and most notably the promised protection of the FBI." The judge noted that Flemmi and Whitey had been acquainted, but the FBI had made them "a perfect match."[7] The problem was far more than two bad apples; he believed that more than a dozen FBI officials in Boston and Washington had engaged in misconduct to protect Bulger and Flemmi.[8]

After watching the hearing as a named co-defendant from the jury box next to Flemmi, who had informed on him—as had Bulger—assassin John Martorano decided to make a deal himself—and what a deal it was. He was sentenced to twelve and a half years in prison for twenty murders.[9] Two months after Wolf released his decision, Kevin Weeks was indicted for racketeering and quickly made his own deal. Weeks agreed to do five years for five murders on the condition that he would show the authorities where John McIntyre, Bucky Barrett, and Deborah Hussey were buried.[10]

Frank Salemme made his own deal and saved FBI agent and special prosecutor John Durham from losing a corruption case against John Connolly to the statute of limitations. It was Salemme who provided the testimony, allowing the Durham task force to arrest Connolly on December 22, 1999, one day before the statute of limitations expired.

Despite all this, Billy Bulger, the president of the University of Massachusetts, was preparing for his finest hour in the national spotlight in late September 2000. The presidential debate between Al Gore and George Bush would take place at his Boston campus. The pressing question was whether the press would be distracted by a highly visible crew of state police under bright night lights across Dorchester Bay digging for the body of Debra Davis, whom Whitey Bulger had murdered in late 1981. Curiously, the search stopped two days before the debate; Debra was found several weeks later.

Nine months earlier, in January 2000, the FBI had seized Whitey's condominium in Clearwater, his future lottery proceeds, and everything else they could find. But even though Flemmi had rolled over, they couldn't find Whitey. Instead, the FBI concentrated on hassling three police investigators just before they joined the Bulger interagency task force that had been formed three years earlier.

Seven years into his term as president of the University of Massachusetts, Billy Bulger was subpoenaed to testify before a grand jury. There, he reportedly admitted to talking with Whitey, but said that he felt no obligation to help bring him in.[11]

With Whitey, Flemmi, and other Winter Hill characters gone, new gangs quickly took over organized crime in South Boston. When one Winter Hill third stringer tried to extort a South Boston tavern owner for protection money just after Bulger fled in early 1995, he was told to get lost.

Worse still for Winter Hill was the trickle of yuppies, which began gentrifying Irish neighborhoods in Southie and Charlestown while Whitey was still around in the 1980s. The sprinkling of gentrification turned into a flood in the decade that followed Whitey's flight, forcing the locals to flee or risk being run over by BMWs. Modest three-decker apartments became top-dollar condominiums, and the old bars, including Whitey's old, seedy hangout, the Triple O Lounge, were decorated with good art and air ferns.

The FBI conducted a dog-and-pony press conference marking the tenth anniversary of Whitey's 1994 flight from Boston, displaying his coin collection and other memorabilia found in safety deposit boxes. Still, the agency had to admit that it had no real leads on his whereabouts. Among the thousands of unproductive leads that the FBI agents had methodically processed and rejected were two that might have been productively pursued in hindsight. The information came from Santa Monica, California.

The years rolled on. The FBI celebrated Whitey's seventy-ninth birthday on September 3, 2008, by announcing that the reward for his capture was being increased from $1 to $2 million. There were some victories along the way, even though Whitey was still on the loose. Connolly was convicted of murdering Callahan after an eight-week jury trial that concluded in November 2008.

Through the years, the families of some people killed by Bulger, Flemmi, or their hirelings brought lawsuits against the FBI seeking some $1.3 billion in compensation.[12] Six such lawsuits were tossed by trial courts, and two awards were reversed on the grounds that such families should have known by 1997 or 1998 that the FBI was involved—despite the agency denials at that time.

Somersault

The Department of Justice (DOJ) did some extraordinary gymnastics in the civil lawsuits, successfully claiming that the testimony of lead witnesses Flemmi, Martorano, and Weeks used to convict Connolly in the criminal proceedings should be disregarded as hearsay in the lawsuits brought by the victim's families. The DOJ argued that Connolly had acted outside the scope of his duties.[13]

The FBI went to great lengths to hide Bulger and Flemmi's involvement in the Roger Wheeler killing, even telling his son Lawrence that his mother, Patricia Wheeler, was suspected of being involved.[14]

On the civil side, the deputy assistant attorney general told an appeals court in Boston that the Wheelers' $860 million claim for the wrongful death of Roger Wheeler was filed too late. "No one here was lulled into not filing the suit," he intoned.[15] One high DOJ official later acknowledged that, as a matter of policy, claims by the victim's families should have been handled differently. Even so, at the time the claims were being litigated, the DOJ rejected a suggestion offered by a federal judge that a compensation fund similar to the one for 9/11 families, be created.

Beyond this, the DOJ was sanctioned by a federal magistrate judge for withholding material evidence in the McIntyre family civil action. As a consequence, the government was ordered to pay $700,000 in attorney's fees.[16]

Celebration

The crowds began to gather on the Third Street Promenade on May 2, 2011, in Santa Monica and cheer "USA! USA!" Whitey Bulger and his girlfriend were not among them. The other world-famous recluse, Osama bin Laden, had been captured and killed. Now Bulger was in real trouble. The Gaskos, as they fashioned themselves, immediately changed their daily regimen. Bulger no longer talked to neighbors or ventured outside unless absolutely necessary. Carol Gasko explained that, more than ever, her husband's health problems were catching up with him.[17]

So were the authorities.

Chapter 9
Boardwalk Empire West

The Flight from Boston

Whitey's decision to disappear permanently on January 5, 1995, after hearing that Stevie Flemmi had been arrested, was not a sudden whim. Both Bulger and Flemmi had been warned by John Connolly through Kevin Weeks on December 23, 1994. Bulger had been preparing for this situation for many years. He was no fool and had long realized that he was a prime target, not only for any gangster who discovered his treachery but also for any cop who couldn't be bought. He must have suspected that there would be a reward offered for him from the federal government, and the rich prize would draw more eager betrayers.

He had laid the groundwork for his disappearance long before he departed. He stashed cash and other assets in both the US and the UK. Whitey even created a whole new persona for himself as a man named Thomas A. Baxter. He had traveled across Europe with his long-term squeeze Teresa Stanley, renting safety deposit boxes in Venice, London, and Dublin.

Once Whitey's long-time confidant Kevin Weeks called Whitey on December 23, 1994, Whitey left with Teresa and went on the run. Althouth Weeks also told Flemmi later that evening, Flemmi paid no attention, since his state police source, Richard Schneiderhan, said there was nothing to worry about.

Flemmi walked out of his son's soon-to-be-opened restaurant in the Boston financial district on the evening of January 5, 1995, right into a trap. With a gun in his face, he sneered, "What is this, a grandstand play?" Maybe it was, but Flemmi was off to jail for a very long time. His inside information from Schneiderhan wasn't that reliable after all. Weeks heard about the arrest from Flemmi's brother, a cop, and quickly paged Bulger.

Whitey had fled with Teresa eleven days earlier, on Christmas Eve, thinking that they might be able to return. Although Teresa was not thrilled about leaving her children and grandchildren behind, they drove four hours to New York City, where they spent the night before driving down to New Orleans and on to Clearwater, Florida.

While in Clearwater, Whitey visited his safety deposit box and bought a condominium in his own name. He didn't pull his trump card — or rather, his false ID card.

According to some accounts, they drove west, visiting the Grand Canyon and San Francisco, until Teresa decided that she had had enough of life on the run. However, it is more likely that they stayed under the radar in Florida through New Year's Day and then headed north.

Whitey heard about Flemmi's arrest on the radio when they were driving through Connecticut. Then, he became Thomas F. Baxter of Selden, New York, an identity he had assumed on the sly almost sixteen years earlier and buttressed with driver's licenses from both New York and Massachusetts. He even had a lodge membership card.

John Martorano, on the other hand, was soon arrested in Boca Raton, Florida, where he'd been hiding from the FBI in plain sight.

By February, Teresa was tired of life on the run and wanted to go home to her family. Whitey didn't fight her. Instead, he made a phone call to Kevin Weeks and made some arrangements. They drove back north, and after one last night together, he pulled into a Chili's restaurant parking lot in Hingham, Massachusetts, outside of Boston and dropped Teresa off. "I'll see you," he said.

Whitey had already acquired a new black Mercury Marquis and had another South Boston girlfriend picked out for the next road trip. She was forty-two-year-old Catherine Greig. Whitey had murdered her brother-in-law some twenty years before, but this didn't seem to bother her. Whether she knew about the killing or not, Catherine was quite willing to hit the road with Whitey. Kevin Weeks drove Catherine out to Malibu Beach in Dorchester, where she and Whitey would meet and travel on as Tom and Helen Baxter.[1]

Billy Bulger had quite a different schedule that year; he had his picture taken with President Clinton, US Sen. John Kerry, and Theresa Heinz Kerry. Then, out of the blue, the FBI had asked him to contact the agency if Whitey called him—but when Whitey called, he didn't alert the FBI. Instead, the brothers talked briefly and Billy wished him well.

Whitey and Catherine would not surface again for more than sixteen years. Meanwhile, the search for Whitey went on relentlessly, fed by reports of sightings all over the world, even as far away as Uruguay.

During the first two years, the FBI said, the fugitive task force dealt with some sixteen hundred "leads" worldwide. All were investigated and all led nowhere. Ultimately, there would be Bulger sightings in more than twenty-five nations to no avail. But the pursuers would not quit. They put a $1 million reward on Whitey's head, a bonanza guaranteed to invite hundreds of calls.

Nearly seven years had passed, but Whitey was still angry about the *Boston Globe* stories nailing him as an informant. Early on, Whitey placed a call to John Morris, who had given John Connolly all those stellar performance appraisals. Morris had been transferred to Quantico, Virginia, and eventually became the director of training at the FBI academy. "You were the one who tried to get me killed with the story," Bulger groused. He continued, "You were my paid informant. . . . You took money from me, and if I go to jail, you're going to jail." The phone went silent as Morris had the heart attack that put him in the hospital. While on the emergency room table, he died twice before being revived. "That must have been some phone call," Connolly chuckled later.[2]

For years, Whitey Bulger sightings nearly equaled those of Big Foot and Elvis. Only one report was credible. A British acquaintance ran into Whitey wearing a goatee, first in a gym and later on the street in London's Piccadilly Circus in September 2002. The man said hello, but the other man denied that he was Bulger.[3] The London sightings soon led to the discovery of one of the Bulger deposit boxes; in it, the police found about $50,000 in assorted currencies and a key to another deposit box, this one in Dublin.

Even though all the years and leads yielded nothing, the Feds would not give up. The huge reward itself was an incentive to inform on Whitey. It kept the media busy, too, churning out ever more sensational stories about the murderous fugitive. Whitey appeared regularly on *America's Most Wanted*. It was almost inevitable that somebody would see the show or one of the newspaper stories and pick up a telephone.

A Well-Traveled Couple

Penny and Glenn Gautreaux were the Baxters' new best friends in Grand Isle, Louisiana, a bucolic backwash peopled by fishermen, offshore drilling platform employees, and their families. Tom and Helen Baxter, in truth Whitey Bulger and Catherine Greig, were generous, paying for groceries, a remodeled kitchen complete with appliances, and even prescription glasses for two of their four kids. So the Louisiana couple easily overlooked Tom's eccentricities and crankiness. After all, Penny and her husband barely got by. She was a meter reader and Glenn worked as a carpenter — when work was available.

Tom Baxter wouldn't pose for holiday photographs but would lecture the kids on the importance of doing their homework, exercise, and diet. Cranky as he was, Tom wept when Glenn had to put down a black Labrador puppy the family vet said wouldn't make it.

In July 1996, Tom and Helen Baxter closed the door on their beachfront duplex across the street from the Gautreaux family and told their friends and neighbors that they were headed to San Diego. They actually headed northwest to Chicago. Later, the Grand Isle police chief regretted that he had let a $250,000 reward slip through his hands.[4]

Two months earlier back in South Boston, Teresa Stanley had betrayed Whitey to FBI agent John E. Gamel at the behest of her new boyfriend, Alan Thistle, a small-time criminal and informant. She told the FBI everything she knew. Beyond that, she conducted a fugitive tour of sorts, showing the FBI Whitey's Long Island and Selden, New York, hideouts and even one of his cars.

Weeks spoke with Whitey about the problem, but Whitey was calmer than Weeks expected, simply saying "at least I know" before declining Week's offer to kill Thistle. "Going out with Thistle is Teresa's punishment," Whitey quipped.[5]

"I wish you were dead, look at all the trouble you caused," Jackie Bulger screamed at Teresa. It wasn't much of a greeting, but she wasn't all that surprised. Jackie's job as clerk magistrate of the Boston Juvenile Court was on the line because he had paid safety deposit-box fees, posed for photographs in a fake mustache to help Whitey get a fake ID, and lied about it all to federal grand juries.

After visiting Chicago, Whitey and Catherine drove to New York and boarded an Amtrak train as Mark and Carol Shapeton. The date was July 23, 1996.

Whitey might have been caught that summer. The Massachusetts State Police sprang into action after learning through an informant that Kevin Weeks was going to supply Whitey with a new Massachusetts identity. An intermediary supplied the ID counterfeiter with names that had been preselected by the state police. Yet for whatever reason, none of the names showed up on local law enforcement databases, and the trail went cold.

On September 16, Kevin Weeks met Whitey and Catherine in New York. They both knew that Flemmi, who had been arrested twenty-one months earlier as Whitey fled Boston, was growing more anxious than ever in jail. Whitey knew better than anyone that the time was coming when Flemmi would tell all. He offered Weeks one last piece of advice in this, their last meeting: "If anything ever comes down, put it on me."[6]

Fountain Valley, California, near Disneyland, hosted Whitey and Catherine briefly in January 2000, according to a witness in a beauty shop who recognized Catherine from photographs she'd seen on the *America's Most Wanted* television series.

Back in Boston, the FBI organized-crime squad discussed the Fountain Valley report. Curiously, neither Kevin Weeks nor Catherine Greig had been placed under surveillance when Whitey went on the lam on Christmas Eve back in 1994. When the FBI interviewed John Connolly two years after Whitey fled, Connolly insisted that John Morris had promised Whitey immunity. "I hope he [Whitey] never gets caught," Connolly said, after repeating his story of how Whitey had protected him in an ice cream shop many years ago.[7]

Some wondered why Charles Gianturco was put in charge of chasing Bulger. Even though he was in charge of the organized-crime unit, Gianturco's extended family believed a Connolly yarn claiming that Whitey had saved the life of his brother Nick, also an FBI agent, when Nick was working undercover in 1979.

Incognito or not, Bulger still lashed out in anger when someone crossed him. A Wal-Mart cashier and a waitress in Santa Monica both felt his wrath. He also verbally assaulted a New York waitress for tucking her loose bra strap under her blouse and then using the same hand to serve Whitey's food.[8]

Whitey and Catherine had concluded that Santa Monica had everything they needed in the fall of 1996, nearly twelve years before John Connolly had to face that Miami jury. The ocean, the world-famous boardwalk, Palisade Park, and numerous homeless people — a virtually unlimited population of people who might loan Whitey a Social Security card and a driver's license for as little as a hundred bucks — made Santa Monica a virtual paradise for Whitey.

In Santa Monica, Charles Gaska, a homeless park-bench denizen, was one of the first mentally ill men Whitey targeted. He changed the name on Gaska's ID by one letter and became "Charles Gasko," renting an apartment on the third floor of the Princess Eugenia, two blocks from the beach. The three-story contemporary built in 1959 on Third

Bulger's last home, the Princess Eugenia apartments in Santa Monica, California.

Street (the same street name of Whitey's youth, in fact) was not far from where one of his brother Billy's daughters had lived when Catherine and Whitey arrived. Although the Princess had once been home to generations of art students from the Getty Museum a few blocks away, by that time, a significant number of retirees lived there, many of whom paid cash, as did the Gaskos.

Whitey had morphed from the flamboyant, clean-shaven gangster who took daily outdoor walks into a white-bearded tottering recluse who spent most of his time indoors—bad news for the interagency task force trying to find him.

Rather than spending time on their small balcony with a good view of the Embassy Hotel Apartments across the street, Whitey watched such television shows as *The Brotherhood,* a series on Showtime based loosely on the lives of Whitey and his brother. He considered the character based on him to be "too violent."[9]

The couple didn't go out much, but when they did, Whitey and Catherine dressed impeccably in casual clothes and blended right in at first-class restaurants.

The Armory

Whitey didn't entirely abandon his old life. He hid some thirty shotguns, rifles and pistols within the walls of the apartment bathroom, hallway and his bedroom, covering the gaping holes with mirrors and paintings left there by generations of art students who used to populate the place. Whitey also kept loaded guns, one behind books on a bookshelf and one in his night stand.

He was perhaps the best-read gangster of his generation, maintaining a library of several hundred books, mainly focused on organized crime, war, and military history to supplement his monthly *Soldier of Fortune* magazine. Of course, he collected and critiqued all of the "Whitey Bulger books" written by his former rivals and colleagues, reserving special scorn for Ed McKenzie, who pretended to be a Winter Hill enforcer even though they had only met twice.

The apartment was an eerie place, with pictures of pets but no family members. Bulger's bedroom was decorated only by an American flag and a pillow proclaiming "God Bless America."

From the beginning of their tenure there, Whitey had implemented certain security measures. Most of the windows were covered in opaque plastic and black curtains. The single window in Catherine's bedroom was covered by a white curtain permitting abundant sunshine to filter through. The martial arts dummy that Whitey used for sparring doubled as a figure in a fedora, occasionally placed where it appeared to be looking out on the street. Whitey himself kept a surveillance routine, peering into the Embassy Hotel windows across the street so often that the staff noticed.

The couple settled into a retirement routine of sorts. Catherine handled all appointments, bills, laundry, and contacts with their fellow tenants and neighbors. Several apartment wags noticed their difference in age. "She was young and looked very pretty. He was old and grizzled," one neighbor wondered, "What are they doing together?" A minister who lived down the hall might have overheard Catherine's motivation one day when Whitey wanted her help. "Someone needs me," Catherine said. "I'm needed."[10]

Whitey was constantly on the lookout for derelicts and mentally disturbed men from whom he could buy false identification. He noticed James William Lawlor, to whom he bore a passing resemblance, walking in the park one day and introduced himself. Whitey claimed that he was an illegal Canadian immigrant and paid Lawlor $3,500 to get Lawlor's Social Security card, birth certificate, and California driver's license. They became friends, and Bulger paid Lawlor's rent for about ten years.

By 2007, after eleven years at the Princess, the Gaskos were confident enough in their anonymity to make some friends. Anna Bjornsdottir, whom *People* magazine had called "one of the world's most successful models" some thirty years before, shared their concern for an abandoned neighborhood cat named Tiger, who the Gaskos cared for until he died.

Not long after John Martorano gave his 2008 *60 Minutes* interview telling his version of the Winter Hill gang story, Bulger began writing his own memoirs in Santa Monica but abandoned the effort after one hundred pages, his anger against Martorano dissipated. Bulger described this as what he considered his transformation into ". . . a real citizen."

Getting the Cat Out of the Bag

"Stop talking to her," Gasko barked to Carol one day, soon after the news that Osama bin Laden was dead. He left Carol in the hallway to apologize to a neighbor for him — Charlie's dementia was getting worse. Bulger's caution blossomed into paranoia, and as Gasko appeared outside their apartment less and less, the paranoia blossomed into dementia, emphysema, prostate problems, pulmonary blockage, and assorted other mythical problems that would have been typical for an eighty-year-old.

Meanwhile, Whitey did not know that in May 2010, one year before Osama bin Laden was killed, a new crew began running the FBI office in Boston. Noreen Gleason, the assistant special agent in charge, and agent Richard Teahan did the unthinkable.

"We can't catch him. We need your help." In a non-descript conference room, not far from where Bulger and Connolly had grown up, the Boston office of the FBI asked the US Marshals Service to join the hunt for America's most wanted fugitive.[11]

Although the agents wanted the help, contrary to normal procedure, the FBI refused to simply turn the case over to the marshals. Even so, the chief US marshal in Boston assigned Neil Sullivan, his best fugitive hunter, to the Bulger Task Force. Sullivan admitted the difficulty but said, "He's catchable. He's no rocket scientist."[12]

Sullivan began his Boston assignment with the interagency Bulger Task Force in September 2010, quickly teaming up with Phil Torsney, a similarly accomplished FBI agent from Cleveland. They soon concluded that Whitey was alive and in the United States—and that Catherine Greig was the key.

Low-intensity efforts to capture Greig had begun months before with ads in medical and dental journals on the assumption that, given her health consciousness, she would make appointments from time to time. But now Sullivan and Torsney went high profile. A $50,000 ad campaign targeted daytime shows such as *The View, Ellen DeGeneres* and *Live with Regis and Kelly* in the hopes that someone in the predominately female audiences of these shows had seen Catherine Greig.

And someone had.

Chapter 10
The Gordian Knot

The CNN news feature about an ongoing $50,000 ad campaign, rather than the ads themselves, got the job done. Anna Bjornsdottir was watching CNN back in Reykjavík, Iceland, when she recognized the Gaskos, her friends at the Princess Eugenia who took such good care of the abandoned cat, Tiger. She called the FBI immediately, leaving her phone number (which was garbled), email address, and her assurance she was "100 percent" sure that her friends back at the Princess Eugenia were really Catherine Greig and Whitey Bulger. After listening to the garbled voice mail, Sullivan was relieved to find nothing in the public records at all about the Gaskos — a sure sign that they were in hiding.

On the West Coast, FBI agent Scott Garlola and his partner thought they were tracking down another false lead in the search for Whitey Bulger and Catherine Greig that Wednesday afternoon, June 22, 2011. They were thoroughly surprised when Josh Bond, the apartment manager who lived next door to the Gaskos, identified them as longtime residents of the Princess Eugenia.

When arrested in the Princess Eugenia basement garage, Whitey refused to kneel down into the oil stains he was standing on, but moved two steps to his right, wondering if the FBI agents would really shoot him as they had threatened.[1] Later, when the FBI searched the apartment, they found Catherine, Whitey's one-hundred-page partial memoir, his armory, and $822,198 in cold, hard cash.[2] Later, Whitey lamented, "A cat got me captured."[3]

189

MASSACHUSETTS STATE POLICE

**VIOLENT FUGITIVE
APPREHENSION SECTION**

MOST WANTED

JAMES JOSEPH BULGER Jr.

WANTED FOR:

**19 Counts of MURDER,
Numerous Weapons Offenses
& Violation of the RICO Statute**

DOB:..........................9/03/29
Height:.......................5'-8"
Weight:.......................165lbs.
Hair:...................White / Silver
Eyes:.........................Blue
Complexion:..................Fair
Race:.........................White
Social Security:..............
F.B.I.#:....................69486A
Peculiarities:.......Glasses / Balding
AKA's:...Thomas F. Baxter, Tom Harris,
Mark Shapeton, Thomas Marshall
Jimmy Bulger, Whitey

1994 Photos

WANTED BY THE MASSACHUSETTS STATE POLICE

After a lengthy investigation conducted by the Massachusetts State Police and Federal Drug Enforcement Administration (DEA), JAMES "WHITEY" BULGER, a notorious "gangster" and a major organized crime figure in the Boston area, was indicted in October of 2000 for his involvement in nineteen (19) Murders that occurred throughout the Boston area during his days as an Organized Crime Figure. BULGER is reported to be traveling with Catherine GREIG. BULGER is a very resourceful person and has cash at his disposal. BULGER should be considered Armed and Dangerous.

Massachusetts State Police, Violent Fugitive Apprehension Section

1-800-KAPTURE (1-800-527-8873) or Nights/Weekends (508) 820-2121
www.state.ma.us/msp/wanted/bulger.htm

"HE ESCAPES WHO IS NOT PURSUED" - SOPHOCLES

The end of a long road. (Courtesy Massachusetts State Police)

Tommy Donohue, the son of Brian Halloran's murdered friend Michael Donohue, called David Wheeler in Tulsa at about 1 a.m. Eastern time with the news.[4]

The Smartest Guy in the Room

Before and after his brief initial appearance in Los Angeles, Whitey chided the FBI and others for not finding him sooner. Catherine's periodic public jaunts had been their chief vulnerability. The FBI had not exploited that weakness as soon as they could have, according to Bulger, who, like his victim Roger Wheeler, was always "the smartest guy in the room." The trip to LA and on to Boston was a virtual debriefing in which Whitey reviewed his fugitive strategy, tactics, and everything the FBI missed. He also exonerated Catherine and Connolly, but opined that John Morris belonged in jail.[5]

Plymouth

"Wish I was back in Alcatraz," the old man complained. Prisoner 57950 at the Plymouth County Correctional Facility near Boston, considered by many to be the Al Capone of his time, was in solitary confinement in a cell the size of a cheap storage locker. The only window was a single pane of glass that allowed his captors to observe the Great Whitey Bulger anytime they wanted. And, of course, they could listen to him rant about being used by the CIA in LSD experiments back at Alcatraz and exploited by the FBI in Hoover's war on the Italian Mafia.[6]

According to some accounts, Whitey saw his captivity in epic, even literary, terms, identifying with Philip Nolan, the protagonist in the Edward Everett Hale short story "Man Without a Country," or Robert Stroud as portrayed in the film *Birdman of Alcatraz*. Even more poetically, Whitey reportedly saw himself as confronted by an impossible task. He calls this dilemma "My Gordian's Knot," (sic) ruminating that, "I'll probably die in this cell."[7]

Yet he is the most fastidious caretaker of his own legend, claiming that more Alcatraz tourists now ask about him than Al Capone. He has insisted in letters to his old Alcatraz friend Richard Sunday that, "I never killed any women," nor, Whitey said, was he an informant.[8]

Catherine Greig had no such illusions. She quickly pleaded guilty to helping Whitey escape justice. During her pre-sentencing hearing, she recounted that her drug-addicted brother had committed suicide. One child of Bulger's many victims later remarked, "If I had a sister like you I would have killed myself too," as Greig gasped and sobbed. She was sentenced to eight years in prison and ordered to pay a $150,000 fine. Whitey vowed to see Greig leave prison, adding, "I'll laugh when I leave this world."[9]

Maybe Bulger thinks that his own testimony will exonerate him. On the other hand, he has been waiting for revenge on John Morris, the FBI agent who told the *Boston Globe* in 1988 that Bulger was an informant. In a sense, he is only alive because his Winter Hill colleagues and Italian Mafia competitors who learned about his publicly reported betrayals a quarter-century ago simply couldn't believe that the FBI would ever lower its standards by making a deal with Whitey Bulger.[10] Had mob members believed this to be true, Bulger may well have been killed.

The glory days are gone forever, and, as one wag commented, life in a federal prison is better than a needle in the arm in Oklahoma.

Chapter 11
The Riddle of H. Paul Rico

Ex-FBI man H. Paul Rico never a chance to fully answer the allegations about his part in the 1981 murder of Roger Wheeler or the other alleged betrayals of his oath. In 2003, he was arrested in Miami on Oklahoma murder charges. Rico had been living in a small Miami Shores condo for many years.

He was a very sick man, having had heart-bypass surgery after a heart attack some eight years earlier, and he wore a pacemaker. Rico also suffered from diabetes, atrial fibrillation, kidney problems, and congestive heart failure.

A number of honest, intelligent people have concluded, again and again, that Rico was a crooked cop, false to his oath, and deeply in league with the Boston mob. The Associated Press put it succinctly, quoting an article in the *Tulsa World* of August 13, 2013:

> Other evidence put the crime boss [Bulger] at the center of an ambitious plot by his gang and retired Boston FBI agent H. Paul Rico to penetrate the US, pari-mutuel Industry by taking over the World Jai Alai company. Four of the murders and two of the murder conspiracies of which he was found guilty were related to his gang's attempt to shoot its way into World Jai Alai, which had been purchased by Wheeler, who was the first of four to die. Then Winter Hill associate Brian Halloran and John Callahan were gunned down after Bulger's corrupt FBI handler agent John Connolly, told him the two were, or were likely to become, witnesses against him in the Wheeler murder.

That conclusion was drawn—or at least accepted—by a number of authors who know a great deal about the Boston mob tragedy. There is much evidence to support their view of Rico as the informer and co-conspirator he is usually made out to be.

But there is a dissenting view.

Authors Joe Wolfinger and Chris Kerr, both veteran FBI men, make a logical case that Rico was innocent. After all, they remind us, Rico was not arrested until Martorano and Flemmi had started singing to the police to save themselves after reams of perjured testimony.

Rico was arrested in his Miami home in the dead of night. His wife was appalled, protesting that he would have complied with any police request to appear voluntarily. Even the circumstances of Rico's arrest were enough to raise questions. Only one of the arresting officers, she said, showed any sign of compassion.

Jailed in Florida, Rico's health got even worse. His lawyers' demands for help were largely ignored until, at their urging, a prominent Florida physician intervened on Rico's behalf. Extradition to Oklahoma followed, but Rico was still a very ill man. Rico was able to plead not guilty from a wheelchair, but that would be his last appearance.

He was doomed, in spite of heroic efforts by his attorneys, who tried to get their very sick client a medical furlough so that he could be treated in a Tulsa hospital. Help him regain some semblance of health, their argument went—he wants to go to trial and clear his name.

Their motion to the court was nevertheless denied, as was a subsequent motion to at least unshackle Rico as he lay in his hospital bed. So that is the way H. Paul Rico died, alone and shackled to a bed. His family, which included a lawyer and a doctor; his attorneys; and a host of friends were horrified.

According to Joe Wolfinger and Chris Kerr, authors of *Rico,* they had every right to be. His treatment in Tulsa, they wrote, had made the sick man worse. The cause of his death was listed in the autopsy report as hemorrhage from an overload of blood thinners. That was so, they said, because the staff of the Corrections Corporation allowed Rico to become dehydrated, the blood thinners accumulated in his system, causing the hemorrhage. The authors suggested that maybe Rico's death was caused, at least in part, by gross neglect.

Rico's funeral was attended by some 400 FBI men, which tends to show the opinion his peers held of him. Wolfinger and Kerr obviously agree with that assessment of the man.

H. Paul Rico is roundly condemned by most authors as a renegade cop and a party to murder. Many honest, knowledgeable people take this view.

An endorser of the *Rico* book succinctly stated the authors' view that Rico's downfall as being the result of a "vendetta against the FBI by self-righteous law enforcement people who used false plea-bargained testimony elicited from an informant."[1]

The same commentator, once chair of the World Jai Alai executive committee, called Rico "an FBI hero, the man who brought down the most profitable Mafia satrapy in the country," a reference to the Patriarca crime family of Providence, Rhode Island, and its satellite Mafia operation in Boston.[2]

Rico raises several potent arguments in favor of the disgraced agent. The most obvious is the contrast between Rico's luminous record with the Bureau—especially the destruction of Mafia family head Raymond Patriarca—and the history of the witnesses against him, lifetime thugs and professional murderers. Most notably, those worthies included John Martorano of the Winter Hill gang, who had everything to gain by testifying for the prosecution—and gain he did.

Martorano got an astonishing sweetheart deal—a multi-jurisdiction plea-bargain—in return for his information and testimony, in the end serving only twelve years for twenty of his brutal, premeditated murders. It would have been his style to incriminate anybody he thought the police might have the slightest interest in.

Aside from Martorano's notable lack of anything resembling morality, he knew that the more and the louder he squealed, the better the deal. He is a little reminiscent of Western bad-man Dirty Dave Rudabaugh, who also gave up his comrades-in-crime. As the local paper put it, "Rudabaugh . . . was promised entire immunity if he would 'squeal' therefore he squole. Someone said there is a kind of honor among thieves; Rudabaugh don't think so."[3]

Martorano's deal with the government was not for complete immunity, but it was phenomenal, a shock to many people, especially the relatives and friends of his victims and much of the public.

He and the other major informant, the equally despicable Flemmi, said some things that were patently untrue or at least highly suspicious. For example, Martorano claimed that he got his personal information on Wheeler, including his victim's regular Wednesday golf date, from John Callahan, who had told him that he received the information from Rico.

Wolfinger and Kerr pointed out that Rico had never been to Tulsa and Callahan already knew the information he gave Wheeler's murderers. He had no need to consult Rico. Callahan was conveniently dead, courtesy of his good friend Martorano, by the time Rico was arrested. Callahan would remain permanently mute.

In the summer of 1982, Callahan's body had been found, odoriferous and badly decomposed, in the trunk of his Cadillac. Any chance to refute Martorano's story died with him. Martorano's account of Callahan's involvement remains double hearsay.

A number of honest, intelligent people have concluded, again and again, that Rico was a crooked cop, false to his oath and deeply in league with the Boston mob. That has been the conclusion drawn—or at least accepted—by a number of authors who know a great deal about the Boston mob tragedy.

The vast majority of knowledgeable commentators agree, and indeed, as the Associated Press concluded, on the evidence in the trials of others that there was as much evidence of Rico's criminal involvement, at least as a co-conspirator and abettor of the other major hoodlums.

Thus, the book's case for H. Paul Rico, whose arrest and passing were either the merciful end of a corrupt cop, or the foul, deliberate, calculated destruction of a fine officer and decent man. On the available evidence, especially as time goes by, nobody can know which with absolute certainty.

We probably never shall.

Chapter 12

A Devil's Bargain

The thing about wise guys is that eventually, they aren't.[1]

When the trial began on Monday, June 3, 2013, John Joseph Moakley Federal Courthouse, named for Billy Bulger's political mentor, shone in the morning sun for the fourth day in a row, at the heart of the once grim, dreary, blue-collar district, now designated as an innovation district. Some other things had changed, too. Irish gangs had different competitors. Triple O's, Whitey's old hangout, was a sushi bar.

The Associated Press described Whitey Bulger as a mobster with a "very long shelf life in a profession where that is not typical." Long-time Boston investigative reporter and author Dick Lehr noted that Bulger once had an "early image as a modern-day Robin Hood and harmless tough guy who gave dinners to his working-class friends and kept drug dealers out of the neighborhood." Seth Stevenson, a young Boston journalist who monitored the trial recalled the way Whitey was once almost revered:

> Non-Irish wannabe kids like me—the Jews, the Lutherans, the Hindus—still bought into this weirdly collective Boston-Irish identity. We were Celtics fans, wearing green satin jackets embroidered with leprechauns. Some of us (to our later shame) fancied ourselves IRA supporters.
>
> If there was a human embodiment of our blarney, it was the outlaw Whitey Bulger. Whitey was a near-mythical

figure for a certain subset of Bostonians. He somehow defined our sense of provincial otherness. He looked out for his own. He had his own code. He was proud, tough, and cloistered, just like us.[2]

The trial was expected to have "all the glamour and gore of a TV mob drama." Bulger had argued that deceased federal prosecutor Jeremiah O'Sullivan granted him immunity for his crimes. "Mr. Bulger believes he will have a fair trial if he is able to present the whole truth concerning his relationship with the Department of Justice and FBI, including that he was never an informant," his attorney J. W. Carney Jr. said in an email. His other attorney was Hank Brennan.

Whitey Bulger, arrested in Santa Monica and still angry.

Time had taken a toll on Bulger. His hair was gone, and his beard was white. The principal witnesses against him included his former partner, silver-haired Stephen Flemmi, and their fifty-seven-year-old former underboss Kevin Weeks, who looked like a bloated leprechaun. John Martorano was the third key prosecution witness.

The listed defense witnesses included Whitey himself, FBI director Robert Mueller, who had worked as a Boston-area prosecutor in the 1980s, William Weld, a former Massachusetts governor who had also been a federal prosecutor, and US district judge Richard Stearns, who had been removed from presiding at Bulger's trial.[3]

Seventeen days earlier, on Friday, May 17, 2013, retired Supreme Court justice David Souter and two other judges on the First Circuit Court of Appeals rejected the argument that Catherine Greig's eight-year term for aiding and abetting Whitey Bulger for sixteen years was excessive. The court ruled that Greig's crime was far more than just harboring Bulger. She "helped Bulger keep his outings to a minimum."[4]

When the trial began, the Wall Street Journal described Bulger as having an "alleged reign as the city's most notorious gangster, whose more than sixteen years on the lam have long accorded him near-mythic status."[5]

Bulger had been charged in a thirty-two-count racketeering indictment for participating in nineteen murders, money laundering, and extorting bookmakers, drug dealers and loan sharks. Bulger chuckled out loud on Friday, June 4, after bookie Richard O'Brien described being threatened by Bulger in the 1970s. Some of the jurors chuckled with him.[6]

Seth Stevenson commented a few days later about how Whitey was weathering the trial. "Each time I've glimpsed Whitey over the past few days, he has been completely still, his lips a thin, straight line. His posture speaks of discipline, of patience, of years confined in tiny jail cells. He remains a surprisingly intimidating presence. But these days it's a presence more akin to that of a stern high school principal."[7]

John Martorano lumbered to the stand on Monday, June 17. Stevenson described him as "a porpoise of a man inside a massive suit jacket. His face disappears into the fat of his neck. When he takes the stand today—tinted eyeglasses, polka-dot tie, pocket square—he tells us he is seventy-two years old, divorced, and unemployed. Also, he has murdered twenty people."

But he has capitalized on his infamous career. "He sold the film rights to his life story for $250,000 and will get even more if the movie is ever made. He raked in another $75,000 or so by cooperating on a book with Boston newspaper columnist Howie Carr. The book is called *Hitman*, but Martorano says that the label is all wrong. A hitman kills people for money, something he says he's never done. He says that Carr chose the title because 'he thought it would sell better.'"

Martorano then proceeded to narrate the same story he has told many times, in many courtrooms. Stevenson noted that

> Martorano discusses these killings as though he's reading from a phone book. He's rehashed his criminal résumé for prosecutors countless times before and now seems genuinely bored of his own story. At one point, he checks his watch, his heavy breathing reverberating through the courtroom microphone.
>
> "And what happened then?" the prosecutor repeatedly asks as he leads Martorano through a litany of carnage—to which Martorano will respond, with a phlegmy grunt, "I shot him" or "I took his knife from him and I stabbed him" or "I left the body in the trunk." When asked to explain where he shot one victim (I'd thought the answer might be something like "the HoJo's in Dorchester"), Martorano says, "in the heart." There is no change in his expression or vocal inflection.
>
> The only time he shows any sort of emotion is when he describes his relationship with Whitey, and Whitey's

longtime accomplice, Stevie Flemmi. "They were my partners in crime," said Martorano.[8]

When defense attorney Hank Brennan cross-examined Martorano that Wednesday, Martorano admitted that he lied to his best friend, John Callahan, just before he shot Callahan in the head. "I couldn't tell him I wanted to shoot him." Martorano went on to testify that Callahan had Roger Wheeler killed because he was afraid that he (Callahan) would end up in jail. Within a year, Callahan's plan to buy World Jai Alai had fallen apart.[9]

Seth Stevenson commented on how Bulger was holding up during his trial, attending "every day, sitting bolt upright, ankles crossed, clothed in his blue jeans; long-sleeve shirt; and a fixed, withering stare. A few days ago, I asked the courtroom artist what it's like to capture Whitey on her sketchpad. 'Oh, he's my favorite to draw,' she said. 'It helps that he stays so still.'"[10] In spite of his age, Whitey hadn't lost all of his gravitas. That much was apparent when the prosecution called James Katz, a seventy-two-year-old, gray-haired, retired bookie with liver-spotted hands, to the stand. Seth Stevenson reported:

> Katz was indicted for money laundering in 1992 when the law began to close in on the Boston organized-crime rackets. At first, Katz refused to chirp to the feds. "If I were to testify," he says now, "I doubted my safety. I was afraid. I knew that the people I would testify against"—meaning Whitey and his boys—"could even reach me in jail." (I note that Katz still seems terrified of Whitey, who is right now sitting about six feet away from him in the courtroom. When asked to identify Whitey, Katz quickly waves his hand in Bulger's direction and meets his steely eyes for a nanosecond before flinching and looking away.) But the prosecutor had threatened to take Katz's house, putting his wife and three daughters out on the street [if he didn't testify]. So he talked. And then he and his family went into the witness protection program.[11]

"Whitewash"

Irish gang chronicler T. J. English contended that "for those who hoped that the prosecution of Bulger would be some form of final exposé on the Bulger era, his trial is shaping up to be a whitewash." English contended that "Actions taken since Whitey Bulger's arrest one year [earlier] underscore these claims."

Savvy Boston-area defense lawyer Harvey Silvergate told English that "the US Attorney's office in Boston is not about to let this case out from under its control. Because then details might come out that show a pattern of secrecy and cover-up going back generations."

John Connolly, in prison since 2002, agreed: "The Justice Department is going to do everything within its power to try to make sure the full story never comes out," he complained from a prison pay phone in Chipley, Florida, in his first interview since Bulger had been arrested. In 2008, Connolly was convicted of second-degree murder in the killing of John Callahan. He had been convicted in 2002 of accepting gratuities, falsifying evidence, and obstruction of justice. As for the practice of using criminals to catch other criminals, Connolly was blunt: "Nobody wants to see how the sausage is made, but in the real world that's how it gets made."

English opined that the crucial question about Bulger's trial "is whether the evidence might reveal that Connolly was merely a foot soldier in a much larger campaign of secrecy and corruption that spanned generations." English contended that protecting Bulger and Flemmi became a way of repressing the potentially explosive FBI history of protecting criminals, including two mobsters who committed murders for which other men were sent to prison.[12] Whitey Bulger considered himself a "strategist" rather than a snitch, but his former contacts convened to share their side to the story.

On Friday, June 21, "reformed" professional gambler Frank Capizzi described what it was like to be the target of a hit twenty years earlier: "A firing squad hit us . . . about 100 shots hit the car." Al Plummer, the driver, was killed exactly forty years ago to the day, apparently in a case of mistaken identity.[13]

The previous day, Diane Sussman de Tannen testified about surviving yet another case of mistaken identity attributed to Whitey Bulger that occurred on March 8, 1973. This time, Michael Milano was killed.[14]

When Margaret King's husband, Tommy, came up missing, Bulger told her, "He's probably in Canada robbing banks," according to her testimony on June 25. She was one of the few South Boston residents courageous enough to confront Bulger about her husband's whereabouts.[15]

Former FBI supervisor John Morris testified on June 27, admitting that he had been trapped by attending some ten private, highly irregular dinners with Flemmi and Bulger, which culminated in bribes. The gifts had begun with cases of fine wines and ended with large cash-stuffed envelopes. He tearfully admitted that he kept silent about Connolly's fabricated reports, which diverted attention away from Winter Hill. Eventually, he took $7,000, which included $1,000 for a weekend tryst with Morris' girlfriend.[16]

Morris testified on Friday, June 28, that he became worried that he would be prosecuted in the Brian Halloran murder. Although he opined he had no direct role in the killings of Callahan and Donohue, he admitted telling Bulger's handler John Connolly about Halloran's cooperation.[17] Morris denied believing he had signed Halloran's death warrant. "I thought he was safe."

During defense cross-examination on Monday, July 1, disgraced FBI agent John Morris apologized to Patricia Donohue, whose husband Michael, who had nothing to do with organized crime, had been collateral damage.

"Not a day in my life has gone by that I haven't thought about this. Not a day in my life has gone by that I haven't prayed that God gives you blessing and comfort." Patricia acknowledged that Morris seemed sincere but said his apology was "way, way too late . . . While he's getting his [FBI] promotions, I'm mourning my husband."[18]

On Monday, July 8, the jury heard testimony about how Whitey Bulger drove a souped-up 1975 Chevy Malibu to the Brian Halloran hit. "The balloon is rising" — when Kevin Weeks heard those words, he knew that Brian Halloran was about to be killed and that that Weeks would never escape the mobster life.

At the trial, Weeks testified about one drug dealer who paid Whitey Bulger a $500,000 severance package to retire. Weeks had been described both before and during the trial as Bulger's "planned successor." Weeks refused to identify the second killer in the Halloran killing "because the gunman wore a mask." Bulger remained silent.[19] Eventually, however, Whitey had to have the last word: "You suck!" Bulger yelled at Kevin Weeks when Weeks told the jurors that Bulger and Flemmi were "the two biggest rats" in Boston.[20]

On Tuesday, July 16, real-estate investor Michael Solimondo testified that Whitey Bulger pointed a handgun between his eyes and a machine gun between his legs after Callahan died in 1982, then asked for $100,000. That was the amount that Bulger told Solimondo that he must pay to stay alive, even though it was much more than what the Winter Hill gang had invested in any of Solimondo's construction projects. He paid.[21]

Pam Wheeler testified on Wednesday, July 17, that in May 1981, her father was negotiating the sale of all or part of World Jai Alai. "Fairly quickly, he was becoming disillusioned with it," Ms. Wheeler said. "It was not performing as he thought it should. He liked to do deals." Roger Wheeler had been negotiating a sale with John Callahan protégé Richard

Donovan.[22] The murder of Tulsa businessman Roger Wheeler was "the event that marked the start of James "Whitey" Bulger's reputation as one of the most powerful and criminals of all time," according to former Boston Globe investigative reporter and author Dick Lehr.

> The Wheeler murder wasn't just the work of Bulger and his associates. . . . It involved a Boston businessman and mobster wannabe named John Callahan who was running World Jai Alai in Miami and was worried about Wheeler discovering how much was being skimmed off the profits of that enterprise. And it involved Paul Rico, a former FBI agent who was head of security for World Jai Alai, who gave the killers the information they needed to find and kill Roger Wheeler . . . Mobsters, gambling, business and dirty FBI agents—in that way, the Roger Wheeler murder encapsulates Whitey Bulger.[23]

That Thursday, July 18, Whitey Bulger and Steve Flemmi saw each other for the first time in nearly nineteen years. Flemmi testified against Bulger—when the former partners were not exchanging four letter insults, that is.[24] Flemmi set Bulger off by testifying that he heard Bulger inform on other gangsters "hundreds of times" over fifteen years. None of this mattered to Flemmi, who testified that Bulger sometimes sold out South Boston mobsters, although he mostly informed on Mafia competitors.

Earlier that day, the courtroom audience had been shocked with word that a potential witness against Whitey had been found dead in the woods some twenty-nine miles south of Boston. Stephen "Stippo" Rakes had owned a liquor store—until Bulger forced him to give it up at a fire-sale price.

June 19, 2013, found Stephen Flemmi, who pleaded guilty in 2003 to ten murders in exchange for a life sentence, testifying that Deborah Hussey was killed in 1985 by and at the insistence of Whitey Bulger, corroborating the version of events told in earlier testimony by Bulger's protégé Kevin Weeks. The previous Friday, Flemmi had claimed that Debra Davis's brother, Steve Davis, was a drug user and informant. "That's a lie," Steve Davis had yelled from his seat in the gallery a few feet away. Having taken the stand again, Flemmi retracted the accusation and added, "I apologize for that remark."[25]

Santa Monica-based FBI agent Scott Garriola took the witness stand on Friday, July 26, to recall the events of June 11, the most important collar of his career. "He had a white summer-style hat on, and he was dressed in light, soft colors," recalled Garriola. "We asked him to get down on his knees on the ground. He swore at us a few times. He said he wouldn't get down on his knees because there was grease on the ground. There was an exchange of words."

Eventually Whitey was handcuffed and subdued. At first he gave an alias. Then he gave up the ghost. "You know who I am," he said. "I'm Whitey Bulger." This was one of the first times the court heard Whitey's nickname. He reportedly hates it; lawyers and witnesses have referred to him as Jim, James, or Mr. Bulger. "I asked him if I needed a SWAT team to get Catherine out of the apartment," said Garriola. "That's when his tone and demeanor changed."

Whitey became cooperative. He signed the search consent form as "James J. Bulger," noting, "This is the first time I've signed this name in a long time." He led agents through the apartment, pointing out piles of guns, knives, and ammunition he'd stashed behind walls. There were thirty firearms in total: semi-automatic .45-caliber handguns, .357 Magnums, an AR-15 rifle, a Mossberg 12-gauge shotgun with a pistol grip, and even a dainty .22-caliber Derringer. Not to mention, of course, numerous Social Security cards and more than $800,000 in cash, mostly in $100 bills.[26]

The prosecution rested on that Friday after presenting sixty-three witnesses, leaving observers to speculate whether Bulger would testify in his own behalf. His lead attorney, J. W. Carney Jr., invoked Bulger's right to remain silent over the weekend.

The defense theory of the case was that Bulger was not an informant. John Connolly "fabricated Bulger's FBI file in order to advance his own career at a time when bringing down the Mafia was a national priority for the FBI."

Robert Fitzpatrick, a retired FBI supervisor, opened the Bulger defense on Monday, July 29, by testifying that he had recommended in 1981 that, once again, Bulger be closed as an informant, as Bulger had been in 1975. "Basically, he was not giving me any information I was out trying to get." Fitzpatrick had unsuccessfully tried to get Brian Halloran into witness protection two days before Halloran was killed, he testified. However, FBI brass in Boston and Washington declined to terminate Bulger's informant status.[27]

The next day, federal prosecutors tried to discredit Fitzpatrick, suggesting that he had exaggerated his unsuccessful attempt to end the FBI-Bulger relationship. But Fitzpatrick was quoted as saying that "he tried repeatedly to persuade the FBI to end its relationship with Bulger, particularly after Bulger became a suspect in the Halloran and Donohue murders. Fitzgerald testified on Tuesday, July 30, that the FBI officials would not listen. "They obviously felt that Bulger was the guy who was going to bring down the Mafia."[28]

On Friday, August 2, Bulger made his first and final pronouncement during his own trial, complaining to judge Denise Casper that he had received immunity from prosecution from former federal prosecutor Jeremiah O'Sullivan, who died in 2009. "For my protection of his life, in return he promised to give me immunity." Bulger told the judge before continuing. "I feel that I've been choked off [sic] from having an opportunity to give an adequate defense. . . . My thing is, as far as I'm concerned, I didn't get a fair trial and this is a sham and do what youse [sic] want with me. That's it. That's my final word."[29]

The Bulger defense called John Martorano back to testify that Stephen Flemmi once admitted that he killed Debra Davis himself. And with that, the Bulger defense rested.[30] Seven hours of closing arguments evenly divided between the prosecution and defense teams began on Monday, August 5.[31]

Murder Served Cold

When Stephen Rakes was found dead in the woods south of Boston the day after he had learned that he would not be called as a prosecution witness, many casual observers assumed that he was yet another Whitey Bulger victim one way or another. According to Massachusetts state prosecutors, Rakes was neither a victim of Bulger nor his own hand.

The previous day, William Camuti, sixty-nine, of Sudbury, met Rakes at a McDonalds in Waltham, bought two cups of iced coffee and gave Rakes the one with two teaspoons of cyanide, according to state prosecutors. He owed Steve money but pitched yet another deal—this one a total fabrication. Camuti drove Rakes's body around for hours before taking his wallet and dumping him in the woods.

While the Bulger jury deliberated in the gentrified neighborhood once known as Southie, Camuti, a dead ringer for unsuccessful 1968 Presidential candidate Edmund Muskie, sat alone at a state mental hospital twenty-eight miles to the south, pondering his upcoming court date on September 10. He had owed Steve Rakes money—big money, but now he found himself locked up while doctors decided that he had been crazy when he handed Steve some very bad iced coffee. The cyanide probably didn't help the flavor much.[32]

Cutting FBI Losses

Bulger's attorneys "described a culture in which agents

took bribes, alerted criminals in advance to wiretaps and pending indictments, and gave them information about informants that led to their murder." Carney and Brennan urged the jury to stand up to "governmental abuse."

Yet as one law professor said, "This trial was not the forum to expose and condemn that FBI conduct." In some ways, the government was able to frame the corruption to control and minimize the dark role the FBI played.[33]

The Vigil

The jurors deliberated for six hours on Tuesday before being dismissed. They had heard seventy-two witnesses, sixty-three of which were called by the prosecutors.[34] The jury started the Wednesday session by asking for the definition of "aiding and abetting." The lawyers and judge conducted four sidebar conferences at noon, and late in the day, the jury asked the judge whether they had to reach unanimity on all thirty-three counts embracing thirty-two individual acts. The judge advised the jury that their verdict must be unanimous on each individual act, but urged them to move on if they found themselves deadlocked on any particular count.[35]

Some two dozen people, nearly all relatives of Bulger's victims, began conducting a vigil when jury deliberations began that Tuesday. Occasionally, they took turns getting coffee in the courthouse cafeteria as the hours dragged on.[36]

On Monday, August 12, after five full days of deliberation, the jury found Bulger guilty on thirty-one of thirty-two racketeering counts involving eleven murders. A woman in the gallery yelled, "Rat a tat Whitey." He didn't react to that but gave a "thumbs up" to his relatives as he was led away.

Michael D. Kendall, a former federal prosecutor, led the Greek chorus, decrying the way Whitey Bulger had been allowed to use federal agents as gang members. "This was the worst case of corruption in the history of the FBI. It was a multigenerational, systemic alliance with organized crime, where the FBI was actively participating in the murder of government witnesses, or at least allowing them to occur."

"The depth of depravity is stunning—the killing of weak people, the women, the treachery against their own friends, shooting them in the back of the head," said Anthony Cardinale, a criminal defense lawyer who has represented mobsters and who first exposed Bulger as an FBI informant. "It's almost Tosca-esque in terms of the treachery that went on, and in the end, everyone winds up dead."

New York Times reporter Katharine Q. Seelye described present day Southie very well:

> The trial gave a glimpse into a time and place that had all but disappeared into the history books. The South Boston of Mr. Bulger's day would be almost unrecognizable now. It has been transformed from a parochial, working class enclave into part of Boston's booming innovation economy. Old triple-deckers have given way to glassy condos for a new wave of young professionals.
>
> The dilapidated waterfront of Mr. Bulger's youth, where he once imported thirty-six tons of marijuana, is now a showcase harbor dotted with pleasure craft and rimmed by the soaring glass side of the federal courthouse where he has stood trial and his former partners in crime have paraded in to testify against him.

The Verdict

After thirty-two hours deliberating on seven weeks of testimony, the jury concluded that prosecutors proved that James "Whitey" Bulger was involved in eleven murders, did not prove his involvement in seven murders, and could not agree on one murder. Three of the eighteen anonymous jurors later described the two month trial as a mixture of tension and fear. Some jurors kept loaded guns by their beds. A few shook with fear as the guilty verdict against Bulger was read.[37]

They found Bulger guilty of conspiring to murder Paul McGonagle, a rival gang member shot in the back seat of a car in 1974; Edward Connors, who had witnessed a Bulger gang killing; and Thomas King, rival gangster shot in the back of the head in 1975 then buried under the Neponset River Bridge in Quincy. The jury was also convinced by the evidence that Bulger had conspired to kill Richard Castucci, a nightclub owner suspected of being an informant. Bulger was also found guilty of the murders of jewel thief Arthur "Bucky" Barrett and John McIntyre, both shot in the head, and Deborah Hussey, daughter of Flemmi's longtime live-in girlfriend, Marion Hussey, whom Bulger strangled to death in 1985.

Finally, the jury focused on the murder of Roger Wheeler. This was the killing that Bulger told his partners would never go away, and Whitey was right. It was one murder too many, the one that Bulger and Flemmi tried to cover up with the assassinations of Brian Halloran and John Callahan, not to mention Michael Donahue, the innocent civilian.

The jury found that the prosecution had failed to show that Bulger had a role in the death of Michael Milano, a bartender mistaken for either Al "Indian Al" Notarangeli, or Al Plummer, a member of a rival gang, killed as he drove in Boston's North End. Nor were the jurors convinced that Bulger had a hand in the killing of William O'Brien, yet another opponent from a rival gang, killed in a hail of gunfire as he drove in South Boston. Missing too were convictions for James "Spike" O'Toole, shot to death in 1973 as he stood behind a mailbox because he had shot and wounded the brother of Flemmi's partner, James Sousa, in 1974, allegedly killed because he was involved with Bulger in a botched robbery of a dentist, and Francis "Buddy" Leonard, whom Bulger allegedly killed to divert attention from the Tommy King murder.

The jury was not able to determine Bulger's connection to the death of Debra Davis, Flemmi's girlfriend, in 1981, whom (according to Flemmi) Bulger strangled because she knew that they were both FBI informants. Perhaps the jury had been convinced by Bulger's lawyer, who said that Flemmi had a stronger motive to kill Debra because she was leaving him for another man.[38]

Attorney J. W. Carney put on the best face for the verdict of Whitey Bulger, claiming that "It was important to him [Bulger] that the government corruption be exposed, and important to him that people see firsthand the deals that the government was able to make with certain people."[39]

The trial verdict established that Bulger was an informant from 1975 to 1990 and had engaged in fourteen acts of murder or conspiracy to murder, six acts of extortion or conspiracy to commit extortion, and five acts of concealing money laundering.[40] Seth Stevenson filed one last article, giving his final impressions of Whitey Bulger:

> Whitey sat bolt upright all summer at the defendant's table, ankles crossed, jotting in his notepad. Over the weeks, I watched him shrink before my eyes. A mean-faced old man, badly dressed, slight of stature, smaller every day. By the end, I half-expected his white sneakers wouldn't reach the floor and would dangle like a child's. Given a chance to account for himself, he didn't have the stones to testify — he must have known he'd crumple under cross-examination. I hope we'll remember he was scared to speak. And then I hope we'll forget all about him forever. His summer in the spotlight is over. May his winter be endless.[41]

A Stable of Killers

When Bulger was convicted in Boston, charges of first-degree murder, conspiracy to murder, and related crimes pending since 2001 remained unresolved in Tulsa. Flemmi and Bulger had already pleaded out and received prison sentences. Tulsans asked themselves whether Bulger should be brought to Tulsa.

"You've got Bulger maintaining a stable of killers and the FBI protecting them," Roger Wheeler's son David said, after describing Bulger as a "a minnow." He was not reluctant to assign blame. "I've spent my life on this. I was twenty-nine when it started, and I'm sixty-one now. This was a federal operation protecting top mobsters, and my father was murdered as a result. The more you know, the more frustrating it becomes."

Should Bulger be brought to Tulsa? Mike Huff, the detective who has worked with David Wheeler for more than thirty years, disagrees with his friend. "I know it's a complicated decision, but the people of Tulsa who have had to endure this would like to see that happen." Pam Wheeler, David's sister, disagreed. "He's an old man. He's going to die in prison at the US taxpayers' expense. Let him die there. Don't spend any taxpayer money to bring him here. It took this long to come to a partial resolution. Just let it end here."[42] As of August 2013, Tulsa County District Attorney Tim Harris had not decided yet whether to take Ms. Wheeler's advice.

Frank Keating, a former FBI agent, US attorney, and Oklahoma governor who became the third-ranking official at the US Department of Justice in the Bush administration, spoke for many when he said, "The actions of the US Justice Department were disgraceful. It remains an outrage. Martorano should have been tried for Roger Wheeler's death. Anything less was a devil's bargain."[43]

Epilogue

The End of an Era

In 1999, Whitey's brother Jackie Bulger, a relative small-timer, got four months in jail for perjury and obstruction of justice. He had lied at least twice: once about visiting one of Whitey's safety deposit boxes and once about trying to obtain new identification photos for his fugitive brother. He was lucky—the sentence was quite light for two counts of perjury, and at least he was alive.[1]

Georgie McLaughlin survived his brothers but spent the rest of his life in a Massachusetts prison. His brother Punchy survived one ambush with the loss of a hand but later departed this life at the hands of Steve Flemmi. Although most observers chalk up Punchy as one of the last fatalities of the First Irish Gang War, Flemmi has claimed that he was simply obliging H. Paul Rico, who was upset with Punchy because Punchy had called him a f-----.

Kevin Weeks, Whitey's long-time friend and lieutenant, who for so long had led a charmed life, became leader of the Winter Hill gang after Bulger and Flemmi went away but ended up in jail in 1999. Soon he followed in the footsteps of Whitey Bulger, rolling over on his Winter Hill gang associates. Weeks pleaded guilty to being an accessory after the fact in no less than five of Whitey's murders. He and John Martorano became a singing duet: they both helped deliver Connolly to federal prison on racketeering and

217

obstruction of justice convictions in September 2002.[2]

In prison, Connolly informed on a crack-cocaine dealer, probably in hopes of a reduction in sentence, but he dressed it up as selfless virtue. "Once an FBI agent, always an FBI agent," he quipped, "I have never forgotten my oath."

In any case, it wasn't over for him. In 2005, Connolly was also charged in state court with complicity in the murder of John Callahan, even though a federal grand jury had refused to indict him for the same offense earlier. Three years later, Connolly was convicted of second-degree murder.

Johnny Martorano pleaded guilty to twenty murders by his own admission but was certainly guilty of more than that. His sentence was astonishingly low, twelve years in federal prison—a sweetheart deal—in return for the immense amount of information he provided law enforcement, including the location of several more buried bodies. His sentence was reduced by crediting him for time served on the nine-year sentence he got in 1995 for racketeering and race fixing.

Martorano turned informant (he said) when he discovered that his old gang pals, Bulger and Flemmi, had informed on him. His fulsome apology to "any family I've hurt," didn't fool many survivors of his gang killings. One victim's widow called the plea bargain "outrageous;" another only said she was "disappointed with the justice system."[3] Said one survivor, "I'm looking forward to meeting again in the future so I can finally put an end to what you and your faithful friends started."[4] "He is," a Wheeler son said of Martorano, "as cold-blooded as they come."

Steve Flemmi didn't escape punishment, either. In October 2003, he pleaded guilty in federal court to ten murders with a guaranteed maximum sentence of life in prison without possibility of parole. The complex, three-state plea agreement obliged Flemmi to plead guilty to first-degree murder in Oklahoma and Florida for the murders of Roger Wheeler and John Callahan. He also pleaded to perjury, obstruction of justice, and evidence tampering. This was the end of the road for Flemmi, after all the years of brutalizing people and selling out his comrades-in-crime. Like Martorano, he managed to contrive an apology to the families of the people he'd murdered, but years later, the victims' families have a hard time accepting it.

All in all, the whole sordid mess in Boston fit the description given it by a congressional committee. "It must be," they said, "considered one of the greatest failures in the history of federal law enforcement."[5] It was indeed a failure, certainly, but it was made all the worse because the Boston FBI agents told their superiors in Washington exactly who they were recruiting as informants, their crimes, and the likelihood that these informants would continue murderous careers. Much of what they did was directly in contradiction of the FBI's own rules.

The Tulsa police had their own complaints about the FBI's unwillingness to help. The lead detective on the Wheeler case put it bluntly, saying, "The FBI and the US attorney's office in Boston did not help us with the investigation. We were lied to. They had targeted the Wheeler case to not get involved."[6]

One Boston news source reported that the Bureau had two agents assigned to run down fugitive Whitey Bulger, but went to a staff of five or six Washington agents working full time to find out the source of the leaks about the Bulger case. The fox was guarding the henhouse.

If anything good came out of the whole foul mess in Boston, it was the spotlight on the crooked cops in the FBI and local police, largely due to the efforts of federal district judge Mark Wolf, who wrote 661 scathing pages about the corruption.

The Patriarca crime family influence was also greatly reduced; many Patriarca wise guys ended up in the slammer. As two Boston journalists recently put it, "the capture of Whitey Bulger represents the end of an era for

Boston's underworld. Despite the undeniable fascination generated by Boston's crime bosses, few will be sad to see their era ended."[7]

Some Last Questions

There remains the question of whether Whitey and the gang skimmed money at World Jai Alai. A 1981 *Hartford Courant* article alleged just that. The newspaper's first allegations were that the skimming was from the concessions income or the parking operations; later that changed to skimming from the betting money.

However, World Jai Alai was audited after Wheeler was murdered. The auditing firm, which had no prior connection with WJA, discovered no "financial irregularities."[8] Yet another accounting firm had run periodic undercover checks on receipts; it found no skimming either.

These two facts suggest that neither Bulger nor his poisonous friends were skimming WJA prior to Wheeler's murder, although doubtless they had designs on the company as a prize cash cow. Stealing by employees under Wheeler, if any, would have had to be relatively insignificant to escape the practiced eye of experienced accountants.

Two Guys from Boston

Roger Wheeler and Whitey Bulger seemed as different as two middle-aged men in the early 1980s might be. Wheeler had a large, heavily-treed estate in the best part of Tulsa, not to mention two ranches and a home on Nantucket Island that he'd dreamed about as a teen-aged boy serving rich people dinner on Cape Cod. In addition, he had all that money, so much that he had taken a chance buying World Jai Alai in 1979, just to keep some $10 million he made on a $1 million investment from burning a hole in his pocket. In 1979, Whitey didn't have two nickels to rub together, his associates and enemies later agreed.

Yet, their backgrounds are almost parallel. About the same age, they both grew up lower-middle class neighborhoods about sixteen miles and twenty minutes apart in suburban Boston. Business acquaintances considered them both to be loners.

Whitey had grown up the son of a one-armed sometime civil servant in a place where lower-middle class, blue-collar ways were what you expected for your children, usually without wanting more.

Wheeler's father had been a printer and proofreader for the *Christian Science Monitor* for more than forty years; despite his modest income, Sidney Sea Wheeler believed strongly in the free enterprise system, even in the depths of the Depression. He imparted that belief to his son Roger, for whom the free enterprise system was *the* guiding principle, according to Roger's son David. Perhaps this would explain why Wheeler once told a journalist that if a Telex victory in its legal quest against IBM meant a depression, he would rather "let Telex go down the tube." And he meant it.

Roger Wheeler wore pin-striped custom suits to frame his dark curly hair. Whitey's day-to-day faded, working-class garb looked like something from a catalog—Sears Roebuck, vintage 1960—sometimes favoring sports shirts that might draw the female eye away from his pattern baldness. However, Whitey knew how to dress for special occasions, or maybe he got some advice from his brother Billy, who had learned in college how to dress his short but husky working-class bulk. Whitey sported a custom white suit, similar to one worn by Roger Wheeler in the early seventies, a suit that might have been worn by the Great Gatsby.

Roger Wheeler's kids could go to any college they wanted—and did. Whitey's only child had died before kindergarten as Whitey helplessly watched. He hardly ever smiled again.

Yet, as different as the experiences of Whitey Bulger and Roger Wheeler were, there were some things they had in common. Neither of them had many friends. They were both slim men who shared an interest in staying fit. They both watched their weight, although only Whitey bought nearly everything he ate at health food stores. They both cared about their immediate families as well as the protection and welfare of domestic animals. Whitey was widely read, perhaps more like his brother Billy than Roger Wheeler, but he shared one fundamental characteristic with both. Roger Wheeler, Whitey Bulger, and Bulger's brother Billy were intense, purpose-driven individuals throughout their careers.

To Roger, that meant engineering school, the oil business, computers, and eventually the cash-rich state-licensed gambling business as well as a leadership position among computer executives aggressively competing with IBM. For Whitey, that meant starting as a lowly "tailgater," stealing merchandise from trucks. He went on to bank robbery and a fourteen-year mid-level gang career after getting out of Alcatraz prison, and, finally, leadership of the most powerful Irish mob in Boston. At the height of his career, Whitey decided who did what in Boston organized crime, in those areas where the Mafia did not reign.

Perhaps Whitey and Roger each succeeded as they did in part because they dealt with business problems directly, bluntly, and as quickly as possible, although both could be cautious when it suited their purpose.

Of course, unlike Wheeler, Whitey Bulger murdered at least twenty people or, at the very least, had a hand in those deaths, if a variety of witnesses are to be believed. Bulger and Wheeler both used intimidation in matters of business. One Oklahoma attorney who litigated a real estate dispute with Wheeler later remembered staring across a table at him and being told "lawyers like you are a dime a dozen." Whitey would undoubtedly have agreed, except where his brother Billy was concerned. One leading Oklahoma lawyer who had every reason to know dryly characterized Wheeler's business methods as "less than amiable." According to a 1981 FBI report, "Some of Wheeler's business ethics were questionable; for example Wheeler in the past hired engineers from IBM or other high technology companies at a substantial increase in salary and with an implied promise of long-term employment. After 6 to 8 months, when Wheeler learned from the expertise of the new employee, he [the engineer] would be fired. Due to business practices as described, Wheeler is generally regarded as having a large number of enemies."[9]

Wheeler did, in fact, terminate or, in the words of one former Telex employee, "whack" engineers lured away from IBM once they had finished the product they were hired to develop. Although the more common industry practice was to retain such engineers to further improve a particular computer product once it was initially developed, Roger Wheeler was hardly the only computer executive who ordered layoffs once particular projects were completed.

Yet Wheeler's sharp elbows in business were, to some degree, counterbalanced by his extensive commitments to charity. Although, as one golfing partner noted on the day of his death, Wheeler chose to do most of his charity privately and without fanfare, he donated thousands of dollars to the First Presbyterian Church of Tulsa, whose associate pastor was a friend.

Roger Wheeler and Whitey Bulger climbed to the top of their respective industries, but in May 1981, the latter succumbed to a temptation he knew he should have resisted. He decided Roger Wheeler's earthly destiny by sanctioning his assassination.

It was a very bad call for Bulger—he got nothing from it but trouble.

When Whitey was captured in Santa Monica in June 2012, he had $822,198 squirreled away in a wall, but so far as is known, it was all extracted as protection money for drug operations or gambling. None of it was skimmed from Wheeler's jai alai operations. In fact, the 1981 murder plot against Roger Wheeler had been a financial failure, as, in the end, was Whitey Bulger's entire career.

Roger Wheeler is buried two miles from the place where he made his fortune. A children's church camp is also nearby, along with a chapel that Wheeler had built in honor of his friend Rev. Bryant M. Kirkland, shaded by tall oaks that bend gracefully in the Oklahoma wind. The chapel is not far from the baseball diamonds and pool that Roger also built—places where, on a summer's day, children can play, laugh, and dream beneath a bold, blue Western sky.

Notes

Prologue
1. Posner.

Chapter 1
1. Posner.
2. *Tulsa Tribune,* May 28, 1981.
3. *Tulsa World,* May 28, 1981.
4. *Tulsa Tribune,* May 28, 1981.
5. Carr, *Brothers Bulger,* 161.
6. Roger Wheeler as quoted by the Associated Press, May 28, 1981.
7. *Tulsa World,* May 28, 1981.
8. *New York Times,* May 29, 1981.
9. *New York Times,* May 29, 1981.
10. *Tulsa Tribune,* May 28, 1981.
11. *New York Times,* June 4, 1981.
12. Carr, *Brothers Bulger,* 160.
13. Ibid.
14. Michael Huff, interview with Laurence Yadon, April 5, 2013.
15. *New York Times,* June 4, 1981.
16. Graham Greene, as quoted by Howie Carr in *The Brothers Bulger,* page 161.
17. Ranalli, 162.
18. English, *Paddy Whacked,* 416.
19. Ibid., 160.
20. *New York Times,* June 1, 1981
21. Ibid.
22. *New York Times,* May 29, 1981.
23. Huff interview.

24. Ranalli, 186.
25. Ibid., 187.
26. *Tulsa World,* May 31, 1981.
27. *Tulsa World,* May 31, 1981.
28. *Tulsa Tribune,* June 1, 1981.
29. Von Hoffman.
30. Kirshenbaum.
31. Ibid.
32. Cullen and Murphy, 214.
33. Ibid., 215.
34. Ibid., 216.
35. Ibid. Some authors and investigators theorize that Wheeler was killed to protect skim money that Bulger and Winter Hill were already extracting, mainly from World Jai Alai parking lot operations. However, the version of events presented here coincides with the opinion of retired Tulsa Police Department sergeant Michael Huff. The quantity and disbursement of the WJA skim was never identified.
36. *Tulsa Tribune,* July 2, 1981.
37. *Tulsa World,* June 17, 1981; *New York Times,* May 29, 1981.
38. *Hartford Courant,* March 27, 2000. Stanley Berenson bought out a $3 million mortgage held by the survivors of Roger Wheeler in the Hartford, Connecticut, fronton in the spring of 1982.
39. *New York Times,* June 1, 1981.
40. *Daily Oklahoman,* December 31, 1981.
41. Posner.
42. *Tulsa World,* November 9, 1982.
43. *The Wall Street Journal,* December 20, 1977.
44. Boyle and Williamson.
45. *Washington Post,* April 21, 1980:49.
46. Lehr and O'Neill, *Black Mass,* 143-45.

Chapter 2

1. Yeats, W. B., 225.
2. Mickey Featherstone, as quoted in English, *Paddy Whacked,* front matter.
3. Ibid., 19ff.
4. Ibid., 25.

5. As quoted in Miller.
6. English, *Paddy Whacked,* 292-93.
7. Ford and Schorow, 10.
8. Ibid., 81-85.
9. Ibid., 76-81.
10. English, *Paddy Whacked,* 9.

Chapter 3
1. Bulger, *While the Music Lasts,* 21-22.
2. Lehr and O'Neill, *Whitey,* 1-17.
3. Bulger, *While the Music Lasts,* 21.
4. Ibid., 18-19, 31-32.
5. Ibid., 38-39.
6. Carr, *Brothers Bulger,* 41.
7. Bulger, *While the Music Lasts,* 31.
8. Lehr and O'Neill, *Black Mass,* 364.
9. Carr, *Hitman,* 422.
10. Ibid., 421.
11. Weeks, 89.
12. Carr, *Brothers Bulger,* 31.
13. Ibid., 45.
14. Cullen and Murphy, 284.
15. Ibid., 184.
16. Martini and Keratsis, 32.
17. Ibid., 29.
18. Ibid., 36.
19. Ibid., 39.
20. Ford and Schorow, 123.
21. Martini, 48.
22. Ibid., 57.
23. Ibid., 50.
24. Carr, *Brothers Bulger,* 64.
25. Weeks and Karas, 171.
26. Nee, Farrell, and Blythe, 164.
27. Shelley Murphy.
28. Ford and Schorow, 122.
29. English, *Paddy Whacked,* 425.
30. Carr, *Hitman,* 256-258; and Carr, *Brothers Bulger,* 108.

31. Carr, *Hitman*, 16-17.
32. Ibid., 215-18.
33. Carr, *Brothers Bulger*, 41.
34. Martini, 101.

Chapter 4
1. *New York Times*, May 29, 1981.
2. Ranalli, 156-57.
3. *Peterborough (NH) Transcript*, October 25, 1973; *Monadnock (NH) Ledger-Transcript*, March 20, 2003.
4. Some accounts also say that he briefly attended Massachusetts Institute of Technology, which has no available record of such attendance.
5. *New York Times*, May 29, 1981.
6. Ranalli, 156-158.
7. *New York Times*, June 1, 1981. Extant Tulsa business directories of that era reflect that Wheeler was secretary-treasurer of the Pipeline Maintenance Corporation in 1950 and president of the Standard Magnesium Corporation the next year.
8. *New York Times*, May 29, 1971.
9. *Church Production Magazine*, Sept./Oct. 2003.
10. Lundell.
11. *Forbes*, "Red Hot."
12. Ibid
13. Lundell.
14. *Forbes*, "Red Hot."
15. Ibid.
16. *Tulsa Tribune*, May 29, 1981.
17. Rodgers.
18. *New York Times*, June 1, 1981.

Chapter 5
1. Goulden, 174.
2. *New York Times*, September 18, 1973.
3. *Forbes*, "Windfall." Only one of the 1973 big five is in business in 2013: IBM.
4. Beman.

5. *Computerworld,* "End Comes."
6. Lundell.
7. "Managing during a major lawsuit," *BusinessWeek,* February 17, 1975.
8. Lundell.
9. Alan Holt, interview with the author, January 18, March 6, and March 7, 2012.
10. Lundell.
11. *Tulsa Tribune,* February 15, 1975.
12. Lundell.
13. Malik, 107.
14. *Computerworld.*
15. *Forbes,* "You Can't Win."
16. Holmes and Wiseman.
17. Lundell.
18. Ibid.
19. Goulden, 179.
20. Loeb, Rhoades, and Company report, as quoted in Goulden, 181.
21. Analysis of Goldman Sachs, June 3, 1971, as quoted in Goulden, 183, 312.
22. Ibid., 193.
23. Ibid., 195.
24. Malik, 107.
25. Goulden, 201.
26. Ibid., 203.
27. Ibid., 210-11.
28. Ibid., 212.
29. Ibid., 222.

Chapter 6

1. Shea and Harmon, 19.
2. Carr, *Hitman,* 319.
3. Ranalli, 171.
4. Carr, *Brothers Bulger,* 161.
5. Cullen and Murphy, 236.
6. Ranalli, 202.
7. Ibid., 207.
8. Ibid., 269-70.

9. Ibid.
10. Ibid., 285.
11. Ibid., 377.
12. Ibid., 401.
13. Carr, *Brothers Bulger*, 217.
14. Ibid., 89.
15. Ibid., 114.
16. Ibid., 310.
17. Ranalli, 165.
18. Carr, *Brothers Bulger*, 190-91.
19. Ranalli, 6-7, 10.
20. Ranalli, 22-24.
21. Other Irish mob sources have speculated that Halloran may have spotted Jimmy Mantville, who resembled Flynn and was with Bulger during the hit.
22. Ranalli, 202.
23. Ibid.
24. Ibid., 25.
25. Ibid., 37.
26. Cullen and Murphy, 246.
27. Ford and Schorow, 10, 22, 47, 119, 129.
28. Carr, *Brothers Bulger*, 131-32.
29. Ibid.
30. Ranalli, 227-28.
31. Lehr and O'Neill, *Black Mass*, 143.
32. Carr, *Brothers Bulger*, 138.
33. Carr, *Hitman*, 309.
34. Cullen and Murphy, 291.

Chapter 7

1. Cullen and Murphy, 105-8.
2. Johnston, 300, 312.
3. *Tulsa World*, December 2, 2003.
4. Michael Huff to Joseph Tauro, US district judge, 14 September, 2002.
5. Cullen and Murphy, 219.
6. Ibid., 222.
7. Kevin Weeks, testimony at John Connolly racketeering trial in US District Court, Boston, May 14, 2002.

8. Cullen and Murphy, 230.
9. Kevin Weeks testimony.
10. Cullen and Murphy, 233.
11. Ibid., 234.
12. Ibid., 238.
13. Ibid., 240.
14. Ibid., 284.
15. Ibid., 287.
16. Ibid., 288.
17. Carr, *Brothers Bulger*, 254.
18. Cullen and Murphy, 296.

Chapter 8

1. Bulger, *While the Music Lasts*, 327-28.
2. Carr, *Brothers Bulger*, 2.
3. Ibid, 2.
4. Shea, 121.
5. Ibid., 124.
6. Cullen and Murphy, 314.
7. Judge Mark Wolf, decision in *United States v. Salemme et al.*, September 19, 1999.
8. Cullen and Murphy, 341.
9. Ibid., 342.
10. Ibid., 344.
11. William Bulger remarks to the media, June 2, 2003.
12. Cullen and Murphy, 387.
13. Thomas M. Bundy, argument before the First Circuit Court of Appeals, Boston, March 2, 2004.
14. Cullen and Murphy, 389.
15. Ibid.
16. Ibid., 395.
17. *Santa Monica (CA) Lookout*, May 3, 2011.

Chapter 9

1. Cullen and Murphy, 221-22.
2. Ibid., 320-21.
3. Associated Press, "Bulger Sighted in London."

4. Cullen and Murphy, 327.

5. Ibid., 329-30.

6. Ibid., 333-34.

7. FBI agent Walter J. Steffens Jr., testimony in US District Court, Boston, August 11, 1998.

8. Cullen and Murphy, 325, 330.

9. Ibid., 364.

10. Ibid., 370-71.

11. Cullen and Murphy, 402.

12. Ibid., 404.

Chapter 10

1. Cullen and Murphy, 410.

2. FBI special agent Philip J. Torsney, affidavit in *United States v. Catherine E. Greig,* June 2, 2012.

3. Cullen and Murphy, 406.

4. Ibid., 411.

5. Ibid., 413.

6. Ibid., 414.

7. Ibid., 415.

8. Ibid., 413.

9. Ibid., 420, 422.

10. Ibid., 428.

Chapter 11

1. *Tulsa World,* January 16, 2004.

2. Alan Trustman, as quoted in Wolfinger and Kerr with Seper.

3. *Kinsley (KS) Graphic,* June 22, 1878.

Chapter 12

1. *Tulsa World,* "Bad Fella."

2. Stevenson.

3. *Tulsa World,* "Long-Awaited."

4. Lavoie, "8-Year Term."

5. *Wall Street Journal.*

6. Associated Press, "'Rent' Payments."

7. Stevenson.

8. Ibid.

9. Lavoie, "Bulger's Ex-Enforcer."

10. Stevenson.

11. Ibid.

12. English, "Whitey's Man."

13. Associated Press, "Bulger Witness."

14. *Tulsa World*, "Survivor of Gang Shooting."

15. Lavoie, "Alleged Victims'."

16. Mahony.

17. Associated Press, "Bulger Attorneys."

18. Lavoie, "Agent Offers Apology."

19. Oppel.

20. *Tulsa World*, "Bad Fella."

21. *Tulsa World*, "Witness."

22. Murphy and Valencia.

23. Watts.

24. Lavoie, "Former Mob Cohort."

25. Lavoie, "Woman's Slaying."

26. Stevenson.

27. Lavoie, "Bulger Was Useless."

28. Associated Press, "Feds Seek to Discredit."

29. Lavoie, "Bulger Declines to Testify."

30. Bridget Murphy.

31. Lavoie, "To Hear Closing Arguments."

32. Grannan-Doll.

33. Seelye.

34. Associated Press, "Jurors Start Deliberating."

35. Lavoie, "Questions, No Verdict."

36. Lavoie ,"No Verdict."

37. *Tulsa World*, "Jury Duty."

38. Associated Press, "'Whitey' Bulger Murders."

39. Feyerick and Sgueglia.

40. Lindsay and Lavoie.

41. Stevenson.

42. *Tulsa World*, "District Attorney Uncertain.

43. Keating.

Epilogue
1. Carr, *Brothers Bulger,* 12.
2. Ford and Schorow, 42.
3. *Boston Globe,* June 22, 2004.
4. News 5, quoted in TheBostonChannel.com, June 24, 2004.
5. *Boston Herald,* February 2004.
6. *New York Times,* 12 June 2002.
7. Ford and Schorow, 150.
8. Alan Trustman, as quoted in Wolfinger and Kerr with Seper, 252-53.
9. FBI report dated June 3, 1981, obtained through Freedom of Information Act request.

Selected Bibliography

Articles

Associated Press. "Bulger Attorneys Grill Ex-FBI Agent." *Tulsa World,* June 29, 2013.

——. "Bulger Forced 'Rent' Payments." *Tulsa World,* June 15, 2013.

——. "Bulger Trial Jurors Start Deliberating Racketeering Case." *Tulsa World,* August 7, 2013.

——. "Bulger Witness Describes Hit." *Tulsa World,* June 22, 2013.

——. "FBI Says Whitey Bulger Sighted in London Last Fall." Seacoastonline.com, January 3, 2003.

——. "Feds Seek to Discredit Ex-Agent in Bulger Trial." *Tulsa World,* July 31, 2013.

——. "'Whitey' Bulger Muders: A Look at the 19 Murder Victims in Former Mob Boss' Trial." *Huffington Post,* August 16, 2013.

Beman, Lewin. "IBM's' travails in Lilliput." *Fortune,* November 1973.

Boyle, Robert, and Nancy Williamson. "The Spreading Scandal in Jai Alai." *Sports Illustrated,* June 11, 1979.

Brookhiser, Richard. "Dancing with the Girl That Brung Him." *New Yorker,* October 28, 1991.

Computerworld. "End Comes for Telex vs. IBM." October 15, 1975.

Economist. "Blast from the Past." July 20, 2013.

English, T. J. "Whitey's Man in the FBI Speaks Out." *Newsweek,* June 18, 2013.

Feyerick, Deborah, and Kristina Sgueglia. "High Life Brought Low." CNN, August 13, 2013.

Forbes. "What makes Telex Red Hot." March 15, 1970.

——. "Windfall for the Little Five." October 1, 1973.

——. "You Can't Win 'Em All." February 15, 1975.

Grannan-Doll, Ryan. "Where Is William Camuti?" *Waltham (MA) Patch,* August 8, 2013.

Holmes, Edith, and Toni Wiseman. "Telex-IBM Pact Leaves Trail of Litigation." *Computerworld,* October 15, 1975.

Keating, Frank. "Devil's Bargain." *Tulsa World,* June 30, 2013.

Kirshenbaum, Jerry, ed. "Roger Wheeler and Jai Alai's None-Too-Watchful Watchdogs." *Sports Illustrated,* June 15, 1981.

Lavoie, Denise. "8-Year Term for Whitey Bulger's Girlfriend Upheld by Appeals Court." *Tulsa World,* May 18, 2013.

——. "Alleged Victims' Relatives Testify at Bulger Trial." *Tulsa World,* June 26, 2013.

——. "Bulger Declines to Testify at His 'Sham' Trial." *Tulsa World,* August 3, 2013.

——. "Bulger's Ex-Enforcer Grilled about Varying Stories." *Tulsa World,* June 20, 2013.

——. "Bulger Ex-Partner Grilled about Woman's Slaying." *Tulsa World,* July 23, 2013.

——. "Bulger Jurors Have Questions, No Verdict." *Tulsa World,* August 8, 2013.

——. "Bulger Jury to Hear Closing Arguments." *Tulsa World,* August 5, 2013.

——. "Ex-FBI Agent: Bulger Victim Foretold His Own Death." *Tulsa World,* July 16, 2013.

——. "Ex-FBI Agent Offers Apology to Victim's Family in Bulger Trial." *Tulsa World,* July 2, 2013.

——. "Ex-FBI Agent Says Bulger Was Useless as an Informant." *Tulsa World,* July 30, 2013.

——. "Former Mob Cohort Testifies Against Bulger." *Tulsa World,* July 19, 2013.

——. "No Verdict: Bulger Jurors Go Home for Weekend." *Tulsa World,* August 10, 2013.

Lindsay, Jay, and Denise Lavoie. "James 'Whitey' Bulger Found Guilty." *Tulsa World,* August 13, 2013.

Lundell, E. Drake, Jr. "Course of Telex vs. IBM Shaped by Personalities." *Computerworld,* October 15, 1975.

Mahony, Edmund H. "Ex-FBI Agent Says He Received Gifts from Bulger." *The Hartford (CT) Courant,* June 28, 2013.

Mano, D. Keith. "The Glass Menagerie." *Sports Illustrated,* June 23, 1975.

Miller, Ben. "Gang Warfare in 18th Century Boston." *Out of This Century* (blog), February 16, 2010. http://outofthiscentury.wordpress.com.

Murphy, Bridget. "Poisoning, Gangster Cases Show No Link." *Tulsa World,* August 3, 2013.

Murphy, Shelley. "Gangster's Life Lures Host of Storytellers." *Boston Globe,* April 18, 2004.

Murphy, Shelley, and Milton J. Valencia. "Daughter of Slain Businessman Roger Wheeler Testifies at Bulger Trial." *Boston Globe,* July 18, 2013.

Oppel, Richard A., Jr. "Former Protégé of Whitey Bulger Recounts 1982 Double Murder." *New York Times,* July 9, 2013.

Posner, Michael. "An Odds-On Motive for Murder: Roger Wheeler's Life Was Ruled by Numbers. And So, Police Believe, Was His Death." *Maclean's,* June 22, 1981.

Rodgers, William. "IBM on Trial." *Harper's,* May 1974.

Seelye, Katharine Q. "Bulger Guilty in Gangland Crimes, Including Murder." *New York Times,* August 12, 2013.

Stevenson, Seth. "The Whitey Bulger Trial." *Slate Magazine,* June 14, 2013.

Surface, Bill. "Racing's Big Scandal." *Sports Illustrated,* November 6, 1978.

Tulsa World. "Bad Fella." August 14, 2013.

——. "District Attorney Uncertain if Bulger Will Face Murder Trial in Tulsa Court." August 13, 2013.

——. "Jury Duty in Trial of Boston Mob Boss." August 17, 2013.

——. "Long-Awaited Bulger Murder Trial to Begin." June 3, 2013.

——. "Prosecution Rests in Bulger Case." July 27, 2013.

——. "Survivor of Gang Shooting Testifies in Bulger Trial." June 21, 2013.

——. "Witness: It Was Either Pay Bulger or Be Killed." July 17, 2013.

Von Hoffman, Nicholas. "A Fool and His Money: Slots and Suds." *New Republic,* June 20, 1981.

Wall Street Journal. "Boston Fugitive's Trial to Start." June 4, 2013.

Watts, James D., Jr. "Writer Chronicling Whitey Bulger to Speak Tuesday in Tulsa." *Tulsa World,* July 21, 2013.

Yadon, Laurence J. "Blind Spot." *This Land Magazine,* March 17, 2012.

——. "Tigress: The Life and Times of Kathryn Kelly." *This Land Magazine*, October 15, 2011.

——. "Where's the Money?" *This Land Magazine*, November 15, 2012.

News Sources

Associated Press

Boston.com

Boston Globe

Boston Herald

Hartford (CT) Courant

Newsweek

New York Times

Oklahoma City Oklahoman

Sports Illustrated

TulsaPeople

Tulsa (OK) World

Tulsa (OK) Tribune

USA Today

WCVB.com

Books

Bulger, William M. *James Michael Curley: A Short Biography with Personal Reminiscences*. Beverly, MA: Commonwealth Editions, 2009.

——. *While the Music Lasts: My Life in Politics*. New York: Houghton Mifflin, 1996.

Carr, Howie. *The Brothers Bulger: How They Terrorized and Corrupted Boston for a Quarter Century*. New York: Grand Central, 2006.

——. *Hitman: The Untold Story of Johnny Martorano, Whitey Bulger's Enforcer and the Most Feared Gangster in the Underworld*. New York: Forge, 2011.

——. *Rifleman: The Untold Story of Stevie Flemmi, Whitey Bulger's Partner*. Wellesley, MA: Frandel, 2013.

Cullen, Kevin, and Shelley Murphy. *Whitey Bulger: America's Most Wanted Gangster and the Manhunt That Brought Him to Justice*. New York: W.W. Norton, 2013.

English, T. J. *Paddy Whacked: The Untold Story of the Irish American Gangster.* New York: Regan, 2005.

Fitzpatrick, Robert, and Jon Land. *Betrayal: Whitey Bulger and the FBI Agent Who Fought to Bring Him Down.* New York: Forge, 2012.

Foley, Thomas J., and John Sedgwick. *Most Wanted: Pursuing Whitey Bulger, the Murderous Mob Chief the FBI Protected.* New York: Simon and Schuster, 2012.

Ford, Beverly, and Stephanie Schorow. *The Boston Mob Guide: Hitmen, Hoodlums and Hideouts.* Charleston, SC: Arcadia, 2012.

Franks, Clyda R., and Kenny Franks. *Tulsa: Where the Streets Were Paved in Gold.* Images of America. Charleston, SC: Arcadia, 2000.

Goulden, Joseph C. *The Million Dollar Lawyers.* New York: Penguin, 1981.

Helmer, William J., and Rick Mattix. *The Complete Public Enemy Almanac: New Facts and Features on the People, Places, and Events of the Gangsters and Outlaw Era, 1920-1940.* Nashville: Cumberland House, 2007.

Johnston, Kevin. *The New England Mafia. Illustrated: With Testimony from Frank Salemme and a US Government Time Line.* Charleston, SC: CreateSpace, 2011.

Lehr, Dick, and Gerard O'Neill. *Black Mass: The True Story of an Unholy Alliance between the FBI and the Irish Mob.* New York: BBS Public Affairs, 2000.

——. *Whitey: The Life of America's Most Notorious Mob Boss.* New York: Crown, 2013.

Malik, Rex. *And Tomorrow . . . the World?: Inside IBM.* London: Millington, 1975.

Martini, Bobby, and Elayne Keratsis. *Citizen Somerville: Growing Up with the Winter Hill Gang.* North Reading, MA: Powderhouse Press, 2010.

MacKenzie, Edward J., Jr., and Phyllis Karas with Ross A. Muscato. *Street Soldier: My Life As an Enforcer for Whitey Bulger and the Irish Mob.* Hanover, N.H.: Steerforth, 2003.

Nee, Patrick, Richard Farrell, and Michael Blythe. *A Criminal and an Irishman: The Inside Story of the Boston Mob-IRA Connection.* Hanover, NH: Steerforth, 2006.

Ranalli, Ralph. *Deadly Alliance: The FBI's Secret Partnership with the Mob.* New York: HarperTorch, 2001.

Shea, John "Red." *Rat Bastards: The South Boston Irish Mobster Who Took the Rap When Everyone Else Ran.* New York: HarperCollins, 2007.

Shea, John "Red," and Michael Harmon. *A Kid from Southie.* Lodi, NJ: Westside, 2011.

Sweeney, Emily. *Boston Organized Crime.* Images of America. Charleston, SC: Arcadia, 2012.

Weeks, Kevin, and Phyllis Karas. *Brutal: The Untold Story of My Life inside Whitey Bulger's Irish Mob.* New York: HarperCollins, 2006.

Wolfinger, Joe, and Chris Kerr with Jerry Seper. *Rico: How Politicians, Prosecutors and the Mob Destroyed One of the FBI's Finest Special Agents.* Longboat Key, FL: Telemachus, 2012.

Yeats, W. B. *The Collected Poems of W. B. Yeats.* Edited by Richard J. Finneran. 2nd ed. New York: Scribner, 1996.

Government Documents

House of Representatives, Committee on Government Reform. *Everything Secret Degenerates: The FBI's Use of Murderers as Informants.* (H. Rpt. 108-414, pt. 3). Washington: GPO, February 3, 2004.

House of Representatives, Committee on Government Reform. *The Next Step in the Investigation of the Use of Informants by the Department of Justice: The Testimony of William Bulger.* (H. Rpt. 108-41). Washington: GPO, June 2003.

Legal Records

Brobeck, Phleger & Harrison v. Telex Corporation, 602 F. 2d 866 (9th Cir. 1979)

Callahan v. United States, 426 F. 3d 444 (1st Cir. 2005)

Davis v. United States, 670 F.3d 48 (1st Cir. 2012)

Donahue v. United States, 634 F. 3d 615 (1st Cir. 2011)

Donahue v. United States, 660 F. 3d 523 (1st Cir. 2011)

Litif v. United States, 670 F. 3d 39 (1st Cir. 2012)

McIntyre v. United States, 545 F. 3d 27 (1st Cir. 2008)

Rakes et al v. United States, 442 F. 3d 7 (1st Cir. 2006)

Telex Corp. v. IBM, 367 F. Supp. 258 (N. D. Okla. 1973)

Telex Corp. v. IBM, 510 F. 2d 894 (10th Cir. 1975)
United States v. Connolly, 504 F.3d 206 (1st Cir. 2007)
United States v. Greig, No. 12-1752 (1st Cir. 2013)
United States v. Salemme, 91 F. Supp. 2d 141 (D. Mass. 1999)
Walker v. Telex Corporation and Telex Computer Products, Inc., 583 P. 2d 482 (Okla. 1978)
Walker v. United States, 202 F.3d 1290 (10th Cir. 2000)
Wheeler v. United States, No. 02-10464-RCL (D. Mass. 2003)

Interviews

Alan Holt, interview with the author, Tulsa, January 18, March 6, and March 7, 2012
David Wheeler, interview with the author, Tulsa, May 6, 2013
Jack Istnick, interview with the author, Tulsa, March 15, 2012
Joel Wohlegemuth, interview with the author, Tulsa, June 2, 2012
Serge Novovich, interview with the author, Tulsa, July 21, 2012
Michael Huff, interview with the author, Tulsa, April 5, 2013

Acknowledgments

When Whitey Bulger was captured, Mark Brown, then managing editor of *This Land Magazine,* requested an article about the Southern Hills murder. This article became "Blind Spot," published on St. Patrick's Day 2012. This was our first foray into the Wheeler-Bulger relationship and the inspiration for this book.

Michael Mason, the founder and current managing editor of *This Land,* has been of great assistance, as have many friends, who have made suggestions and arranged key interviews. These early encouragers notably included Alan Holt, Burt Holmes, Stephen R. Clouser, Jim Millaway (who suggested this transition from writing about Old West-era genre books to modern crime), and Bill McMahon, editor of *Tulsa Lawyer* magazine. Michael Wallis supported us early on, as did veteran journalist Clayton Vaughn, Tony Ringold, Dr. Robert Gold, and Gary and Mary Holmes. As we prepared our final manuscript, Kathy LaFortune, Congressman Jim Bridenstine, and FBI Records Management Division section chief David M. Hardy provided invaluable, timely assistance dislodging FBI investigation documents that we had requested through the Freedom of Information Act.

This is the seventh time that Irene and Larry Chance of Flying Fingers Typing and Secretarial Service patiently and flawlessly prepared our final manuscript for Pelican Publishing Company. Jae Jaeger, genealogist extraordinaire, researched the Wheeler family's immigration to America. Two retired law enforcement officials in the Boston area provided significant background information, as did librarians Mary Moore and Sherri Stanford of the Tulsa City County Library, Rachel Baumgartner of the Reading, Massachusetts, Public Library and Jennifer Nellis of the University of Oklahoma Law Library.

Others who provided significant assistance included Garvin Isaacs, Esq., of Oklahoma City, Mike Nance, Mike Huff, David Wheeler, Kaethe Houst, Jack Istnick, Serge Novovich, Joel Wohlegemuth, Richard E. Wright, Gary Glanz, Russell Dixon, David Dixon, Carolyn Westertvelt, John Brooks Walton, Hon. Paul Cleary, Hon. Daniel J. Boudreau, Ann LaGere, Neal Kirkpatrick, and Ralph Schaefer, senior editor of *Tulsa Business and Legal News*.

Thanks also to writing coach extraordinaire Barry Friedman and the Tulsa Drafters Writing Club: Warren and Lynette Danskin, Maribeth Garrett, Natalie Gould, and Kathryn Brownfield, who reviewed excerpts of the project as it was developed.

Mystery writer James Patrick Hunt; Greg Gray; James Sturdivant; David Crowell; Mike Seymour; George L. Hangs Jr., Esq.; Tom Hinds; Jean Coulter, Esq.; Shawn King; Kyle Bunney; C. J. McMahan; Leslie Mansfield; Eric Farque; Mary Anne McGivern; John Rooney; Richard Lawler; Karen Rebele; Louis Coleman; Jim Barlow; and Mike Samara all either helped or encouraged us.

Institutions that assisted in this project include the genealogy, interlibrary loan, and research departments of the Tulsa City County Library; the University of Tulsa library; the Western History Collection, University of Oklahoma; the Tulsa Genealogy Society; the Reading, Massachusetts, Public Library; the Rice University Public Affairs Office; and the Peterborough, New Hampshire, Town Library.

We are grateful to each of them.

Index